THE
MĒTAVALUES®
BREAKTHROUGH

ABOUT ABRAHAM MASLOW:

"A century from now it may well be that the most important and meaningful proclamations regarding our behavior were not by Freud, or Darwin, or Watson, or Skinner but by Abraham Maslow." [1]

OG MANDINO
author of *The Greatest Salesman in the World*

"Maslow's profound concept of self-actualization could generate a Copernican Revolution of work and society, catapulting us out of what future generations will look back on as the dark ages of management." [2]

JIM COLLINS
author of *Good to Great*

"We have all been quoting Maslow for years … The values and principles he taught decades ago are even more relevant today." [3]

STEPHEN COVEY
author of *The Seven Habits of Highly Effective People*

"… Maslow matters more today than when he lived. Maslow matters because he understood human nature and motivation and self-actualizing performance better than anyone alive today does." [4]

DEBORAH C. STEPHENS
editor of *The Maslow Business Reader*

DREAM & DARE...
A New Life Based Upon All
That is True, Beautiful & Good

THE
METAVALUES®
BREAKTHROUGH

LIMITLESS POWER,
BOUNDLESS OPPORTUNITIES

Abraham Maslow's forgotten discovery

expanded, clarified, and presented

in a dynamic new program

LARRY MULLINS
with L. A. STAMFORD

New York

The MetaValues® Breakthrough
Limitless Power, Boundless Opportunities

Paperback ISBN: 978-1-60037-576-7

Hardcover ISBN: 978-1-60037-577-4

MORGAN · JAMES
THE ENTREPRENEURIAL PUBLISHER

Morgan James Publishing, LLC
1225 Franklin Ave., STE 325
Garden City, NY 11530-1693
Toll Free 800-485-4943
www.MorganJamesPublishing.com

In an effort to support local communities, raise awareness and funds, Morgan James Publishing donates one percent of all book sales for the life of each book to Habitat for Humanity. Get involved today, visit **www.HelpHabitatForHumanity.org**.

For Joan

CONTENTS

PREFACE

Long before anyone heard of Tony Robbins and Stephen Covey, Abraham Maslow, the original master of self-empowerment, set the motivational revolution into motion. Maslow's ideas about self-fulfillment, creativity, and well-being still influence not only psychology, but also modern health care, education, managerial theory, organizational development, and even theology.

However, the concept Maslow called his most important finding, *MetaValues* (or what he designated as *Being values)*, has been neglected and is in danger of being lost. MetaValues are inner resources available to everyone. They change lives. They drive and inspire the top one percent of the world's achievers, people Dr. Maslow designated as *Self-Actualizers*. MetaValues will one day lead to an explosion of human potential that will revolutionize the world we live in.

The above pronouncements may seem to some to be grandiose. They did not originate with me, they originated with Abraham Maslow. I believe he was right. Although you will find many new ideas in these pages, there is no pretense that this is the final word about MetaValues. This is rather an effort to open new doors for further exploration and discovery. Dr. Maslow was convinced—as I am—that when that day comes, MetaValues will foster *"A new image of man, a new image of society, a new image of nature, a new philosophy of science, a new economics, a new everything…"* [5]

MetaValues are a triad of core principles that are embedded in all normal minds: *Truth, Beauty,* and *Goodness.* They are not taught; they are timeless. They are potential active agents that exist independently as universe realities. Yet MetaValues are not mystic fluff—Abraham Maslow was a pragmatic scientist and a professed atheist. Even so, any mature and reasonable theologian would readily embrace the concept of MetaValues. This unifying quality is one of their most remarkable characteristics. They transcend disciplines, religions, and creeds.

For example, with many preconceptions and reservations, I recently sat down to read Christopher Hitchens's book: *god is not Great … How Religion Poisons Everything*. (He deliberately did not capitalize God.) What a provocative, nasty title, I thought. Obviously this was yet another mean-spirited rant by an atheist.

I did not find what I expected. In fact, after reading his introduction to the book, I actually acquired some affection for Hitchens. Unfortunately, he did fail to define religion. (My dictionary offers six different definitions.) He thus was able to lump numerous straw men (formal religious dogma that few people really believe) together with a few serious questions that are asked and investigated by religionists. This shotgun approach permitted him to lament a host of religious evils and excesses that no sane mortal supports, while attempting a mass annihilation of every aspect of human belief in a higher power.

The bottom line seems to be that Hitchens does not believe that religion is a legitimate discipline. Much as did Ayn Rand, he seems to hold that the questions asked by theologians and philosophers can be more effectively answered by science.

Were it not for one endearing passage in the introduction to his book, these logic-tight barriers would render hopeless the rational joining of an issue about higher universe realities with Hitchens. When all seemed beyond redemption, he embraced MetaValues. He did so in a profound and moving way. Hitchens told the story of the funeral of his father. It took place in a historic chapel in England, overlooking Portsmouth. Hitchens spoke from the pulpit and gave a reading from the Bible. Quoting Paul, he said:

> *"Finally, brethren, whatsoever things are true, whatsoever things are honest, whatsoever things are just, whatsoever things are pure, whatsoever things are lovely, whatsoever things are of good report: if there be any virtue, and if there be any praise, think on these things."* [6]

Then Hitchens explained why he selected this passage:

> *"I chose this because of its haunting and elusive character, which will be with me at the last hour, for its essentially secular injunction, and because it shone out from the wasteland of rant and complaint and nonsense and bullying which surrounds it."* [7]

For precisely the same reasons, I chose this passage from Hitchens's own wasteland of rant, etc. Yet perhaps the most important questions to answer are these: Why does this passage shine out for both an atheist and a believer? How is it that people of radically different persuasions and cultures share the same MetaValues of Truth, Beauty, and Goodness? Wrapped up in the answer to these questions is perhaps the twentieth century's most important scientific discovery about the nature of human beings.

Abraham Maslow believed that values should not be the exclusive domain of religionists. He advocated a science of values. Yet he also grasped that MetaValues transcend the disciplines of science, theology, and philosophy. Unlike Rand or Hitchens, Maslow understood that science does not have all the answers. Science can tell us much about material reality, or *what is*. Science can even suggest possibilities, *what could be*. But the poet or the religionist offers a vision for us of *what ought to be*. And science without values builds bigger bombs and more efficient gas chambers. Dr. Maslow fought hard to break down the barriers between science and religion:

> *"I [have] pointed out that both orthodox science and orthodox religion have been institutionalized and frozen into a mutually excluding dichotomy. This separation into Aristotelian a and not-a has been almost perfect … Every question, every answer, every method, every jurisdiction, every task has been assigned to either one or the other, with practically no overlaps. One consequence is that they are both pathologized, split into sickness, ripped apart into a crippled half-science and a crippled half-religion."* [8]

Unfortunately, Maslow was never able to distill his ideas for mainstream readers; he wrote almost exclusively for his peers. The world is the poorer for this, because Maslow uncovered truths about the human condition that are tremendously uplifting and inspiring—and are easily within the understanding of nearly every person on the planet. With this book, nearly four decades after Maslow's death, individuals at last have a program that shows them how to put these truths to work in their lives.

The Introduction of *The MetaValues Breakthrough* overviews the discovery of self-actualizing people and the findings that challenged the assumed ceilings of human potential. In chapter one I show how Dr. Maslow discovered the secrets that drive and inspire the top one percent of achievers, and how the key components of his discovery—MetaValues—were largely brushed aside.

Chapters two through five deal with removing the blocks that prevent the self-actualizing process to operate, and replacing them with the two requisites of success: an impregnable self-respect and an uncompromising mastery of the inner life.

In chapter six, you will learn the new theory of MetaValues genius, MetaThink™, and how to use it to enrich your life. A complete program applying breakthrough discoveries of champion athletes and performers is presented in chapter seven. Chapter eight expands Maslow's concepts and presents a new model of humankind. You will be launched toward full use of your powers with the *54 Minutes That Will Change Your Life* process.

The MetaValues Breakthrough provides tested and proven techniques for capturing inspiring visions of things that *ought to be* and actualizing them into realities. True stories illustrate how ordinary people connected with Truth, Beauty, and Goodness and transformed their unfinished lives from meaningless—or even tragic—to magnificent and unforgettable. Regardless of your age or circumstances, you too can use MetaValues to elevate your life and the lives of those around you to another level.

Larry Mullins
St. Augustine, Florida
January 2009

INTRODUCTION
The Top One Percent

"I think it significant that in more than a quarter of a century since Maslow's death, there has been no sign of a decline in his reputation, whereas Freud's and Jung's are heavily bullet scarred. This, I believe is because there is a sense in which Maslow has not come into his own. His significance lies in the future and will become apparent in the 21st century." [9]

COLIN WILSON

New York in the late '30s was experiencing a golden age, perhaps the most luminous period in that great city's history. While war seemed inevitable in Europe, New York was, as Abraham Maslow described it, "the new Athens." Great minds gravitated there, drawn by the city's cultural riches and the open-armed welcome it offered scientists and academics who fled the Nazi menace overseas. It was a heady time for a man of great intellect like Maslow to become a professor at Brooklyn College. Even with an IQ approaching 200, Maslow found the array of genius around him dazzling.

Two minds seemed to soar above the others. One was Ruth Benedict. By this point, Benedict had published her groundbreaking work, *Patterns of Culture*, in which, through the study of three Native American tribes, she identified how different cultures develop distinct personalities that they pass along to future generations within that culture. The book changed the way people thought about culture and swayed the debate about cultural equality. In addition, Benedict had mentored Margaret Mead, a young anthropologist who had already made a significant impact on the field.

The other extraordinary individual was Max Wertheimer. Wertheimer had developed important ideas on Gestalt theory and, with his colleagues Wolfgang Köhler and Kurt Koffka, founded the school of Gestalt psychology that saw the brain as a holistic mechanism capable of great leaps of thought. He'd been an influential innovator in Czechoslovakia and Germany, inventing a lie detector and developing remarkable theories on movement perception. He escaped the Nazis in the early '30s and he was working on a text that would encapsulate his life's work. (That text became the landmark book, *Productive Thinking.*)

Both Benedict and Wertheimer had made pivotal accomplishments. What struck Maslow, however, was not their level of achievement or their drive. After all, there were many noted professionals in New York at the time at least as driven as the two. What Maslow found remarkable was their uncommon degree of sensitivity to others, their uncompromising integrity, and their passionate devotion to a mission greater than themselves.

Fascinated by what he saw in these two individuals, Maslow studied them more closely. He began to jot down notes about their unique personality characteristics. He observed that, though they were remarkably knowledgeable in their fields, they demonstrated a childlike, creative openness toward new discoveries. They were busy and driven to excel at all times, yet they focused their egos upon tasks and problems rather than personal gain. They simply did not act the way most accomplished people acted—and certainly not the way the average person acted.

Maslow knew that what he saw in Benedict and Wertheimer had implications for all of humanity. The way they approached the world signaled something, if only he could identify it. For several months, he wrote about them in his journal, trying to understand them. He listed their attributes and compared them to the attributes of others. He studied the differences between the two, noting that one was a woman who achieved her Ph.D. relatively late in life after a traumatic, lonely childhood and a difficult marriage. The other was a man trained as a musician and lawyer before discovering his driving passion. She grew up in America. He grew up in battle-torn Europe.

Then the pivotal insight came. Maslow looked down at his descriptions of Benedict and Wertheimer and realized that he was not looking at lists of the qualities of two people. Instead, he was looking at a description of a *kind of person.* The two were different in many ways, raised in different environments, but what was most notable was what united them. Each was more authentic than most people were. Each was fully dedicated to the process of actualizing his or her potential, being the best version of him or herself, and yet equally dedicated to being fully human. Each laughed with gusto, lived on the verge of reckless abandon, and embraced life. Could it be that this is what a human being is actually supposed to be? Maslow wondered. Why are these two people able to reach such levels of excellence? Are there others?

This line of thinking ran straight up against Maslow's Freudian and behaviorist training, all of which taught him to draw conclusions from society's sickest individuals rather than its healthiest. But what if doing so left a gaping hole in the understanding of human potential? What if there were more like Benedict and Wertheimer? What could one learn from a clinical study of these people? Would it be possible to discover the inner forces that drove the highest and best of humanity?

The new idea was electric and overwhelming in its implications. With rare exceptions, psychology and psychiatry had examined only the failed—or at least the foundering—specimens of humankind. But that evening in Brooklyn, Abraham Maslow uncovered evidence of a new kind of person: the *self-actualizing* individual. This discovery would launch an avocation to find more of the people somehow engaged in the process of making their latent and potential selves real. Eventually it would become a relentless, glorious obsession and it would set into motion a new school of psychology. Third Force psychology would challenge old-school ideas with the revolutionary concept of self-actualization. It would lead Maslow to discover significant evidence that concealed within every normal human being is the nucleus of a potential superior self. It was a genuine breakthrough.

And it would be largely unacknowledged.

For the next thirty years of his life, Maslow studied this new paradigm of human potential endlessly. In 1943, he presented a paper that featured his Hierarchy of Human Needs. This would turn out to be the one piece of his work that nearly all his academic peers in psychology enthusiastically embraced. He identified five levels of human desires and requirements. With the first four (termed deficiency needs), a person feels virtually nothing if these needs are satisfied, but anxious if they are missing. The fifth level was different, though. Maslow termed this highest level of the pyramid, Being needs or B-needs. This was the level of self-actualization. This was what Maslow saw in Benedict and Wertheimer. This fifth level made us the best we could be.

The development of the Hierarchy led Maslow to delve even deeper into the study of Self-Actualizers and into what he termed metamotivations. Yet the more he did so, the more the academic establishment resisted him. He was a threat to the status quo—upsetting the apple cart of Freudian and behaviorist psychology—and few chose to follow him along this path. Still, Maslow did not go quietly. In a 1950 paper, he declared, "It becomes more and more clear that the study of crippled, stunted, immature, and unhealthy specimens can yield only a cripple psychology and a cripple philosophy. The study of self-actualizing people must be the basis for a more universal science of psychology." [10]

Rather than rally his contemporaries, though, this paper distanced them further. In their eyes, his new theories were too radical. His Third Force psychology not only challenged the established and profitable Freudian and behaviorist schools, it overran the customary barriers that insulated the disciplines of science, philosophy, and religion in comfortable, logic-tight compartments. There was general agreement in traditional schools of psychology that Maslow had lost it, that he made his only real contribution to science (the Hierarchy) early in his career.

Maslow continued his work throughout the '50s and '60s, but if you were to examine the leading intellectual magazine literature of that time, you would not find him there. Maslow had identified a kind of human being—an individual whose life was passionately devoted to a mission or cause greater than self—and something else: B-values. These values he described as the ultimate values which cannot be reduced to anything more ultimate, primarily Truth, Beauty, and Goodness. It was a model to which all of humanity could aspire, but it remained, as he termed it, the unnoticed revolution.[11]

A frustrated Dr. Maslow turned to business organizations and management as a real-world testing ground for his theories. The management of Saga Foods Corporation of Menlo Park, California, embraced his ideas and applied them to their company. They were so thrilled with the results that they offered him a fellowship. Maslow wrote to British philosopher Colin Wilson about his success there, saying, "[Saga Foods is run with] an effort to appeal to the very highest in human nature, and to set up a work situation in which self-actualization and personal growth become more possible. And in which, as a kind of a by-product—a synergistic by-product—they simply do a good job. It makes a better team. Everybody is both happier and more efficient. If America sweeps the world, *this* is the way it is going to sweep the world." [12]

A reenergized Maslow saw the business community as a platform from which to launch his theories to the mainstream, bypassing the academic establishment. Sadly, time ran out for him. He died suddenly in Menlo Park on June 8, 1970, at the age of sixty-two.

Although death cut off his work so abruptly, Dr. Maslow left many threads for others to pick up and develop. For more than twenty years, I have sought to unravel and follow these threads. Using the works of Maslow and other great thinkers as a foundation, I have hammered out many original and easy-to-use tools for assisting the life-changing self-empowerment of all kinds of people. These methods have been presented to everyone from corporate executives to U.S. Air Force officers to high school seniors. Most people not only understand them easily, but also adopt them readily.

In my work as a consultant, I have been able to marry the management concepts Maslow developed near the end of his life with modern ideas. Like Maslow, I have used them to help business organizations grow and prosper. Yet, I've learned that success in such an environment depends on continuous superlative leadership at the top. Sadly, that quality of leadership is much too rare. I am now convinced that, as important as enlightened organizations are, our greatest need as a society is the progress and enlightenment of the individual. The revolution that Abraham Maslow envisioned must spring from the grassroots rather than wait for inspiration and direction to trickle down from the top.

Over the years, I have discovered that modern minds have trouble applying the classical terms of Truth, Beauty, and Goodness to the hard practicalities of life. In order to make these ideas more accessible, I have chosen to supplement them with the reasonably parallel—and more action-related—terms Integrity, Excellence, and Caring. While we cannot see or examine a MetaValue, we can detect its presence and influence in the same way Dr. Maslow did. When he observed a Self-Actualizer living a life of remarkable *Integrity*, he deducted that the MetaValue of Truth was influencing that life. When he detected *Excellence*, he concluded that this was an expression of the MetaValue of Beauty. A *Caring* individual is one expressing the MetaValue of Goodness. The terms Integrity, Excellence, and Caring represent the MetaValues of Truth, Beauty, and Goodness made visible through action.

MetaValues are not something someone created; they are realities that were discovered. The best evidence for this is the fact that all normal people, regardless of race, religion, or culture, share and recognize MetaValues on some level. I learned that even the most materialistic business people, perplexed by the challenge of applying MetaValues to their work, readily respond when asked, "Would you hire an associate you knew to be lacking in Integrity? How about one who was uncaring and indifferent about his fellow workers, customers, and the community in general? Would you want to employ people who could not be motivated to strive for high levels of Excellence in their work?" The answers to these questions are so obvious because MetaValues are universal realities that transcend cultures and the barriers between science, philosophy, and religion.

In my judgment, we can no longer afford for Maslow's "unnoticed revolution" to continue to go unnoticed. Attempting to navigate through the world without a true understanding of our potential is akin to ignoring the benefits of medical advancements or breakthroughs in technology. This is especially true in times fraught with unprecedented challenges and an equally unprecedented need for us to bring out the best in ourselves. Would we have been willing to forestall the implementation of life-saving vaccinations or the wonders of the personal computer for decades? Why, then, would we be willing to delay the acknowledgment that we can all be much greater than we already are?

I had hoped that someone would write a book that would bring Dr. Maslow's MetaValue discoveries directly to the people. I longed for a book that was true to the fearless, pioneering spirit that drove him toward new paths in human potential. I hoped this book would correlate the science of self-empowerment with some of the highest known philosophical and spiritual insights and present them in a form that people could understand and apply to their lives.

Since no one has written this book, I decided to write it myself.

MetaValues made a remarkable difference in my life. I am confident that they can make a remarkable difference in yours. Dr. Maslow believed that MetaValues would one day change the world. By reading these pages, you have joined in this quest. I look forward with great anticipation to what we will discover.

CHAPTER ONE

MetaValues … The Lost Discovery of Abraham Maslow

"Perhaps my most important finding was the discovery of what I am calling B-values or the intrinsic values of Being … this list of described characteristics of the world as it is perceived in our most perspicuous moments is about the same as what people through the ages have called the eternal verities, or the spiritual values, or the highest values, or the religious values [truth, beauty, and goodness]." [13]

ABRAHAM MASLOW
Religions, Values, and Peak-Experiences

On a beautiful Colorado afternoon several years ago, I watched several brave people leap, one by one, off Lookout Mountain and ascend effortlessly on paragliders into the cloudless sky. As though being lifted by some mysterious, invisible power, they circled higher and higher—the way the eagle and hawk have for untold ages. I knew, of course, that there was no mysterious power operating; rising warm air thermals naturally lifted these bird-emulators. The fliers knew this as well, secure in the understanding that nature and humanity's ingenuity would keep them safe.

As I watched, a thought occurred to me: Long before recorded history, people surely envied the flight of birds as they soared effortlessly on air thermals. Yet, it was not until the middle of the twentieth century that someone created the simple design for the paraglider and built the first prototype. Why did it take so long? People had access to the raw materials to make a paraglider many centuries before. And, of course, air thermals always existed, waiting for humans to use them the way birds instinctively did. The only thing lacking was the design and someone daring enough to leap into thin air to test it.

It dawns on me that, centuries from now, historians will look back at our failure to actualize more of our potential—when all of the "raw materials" are within reach—with an equal degree of puzzlement. They will likely wonder why Abraham Maslow's peers broadly rejected his discovery of the reality and power of MetaValues. They will note that Maslow's other ideas had significant impact on what scientists imagined to be the limits of the highest reaches of human nature. I can't help but believe, though, that they will find it puzzling that, nearly four decades after the premature death of the man who started the self-empowerment revolution, most Americans are still actualizing only a tiny fraction of their potential.

On that bright Colorado afternoon, the themes of this book began to coalesce for me. At that moment, I understood something that you will understand as you read further. We don't need to wait for a MetaValues revolution to sweep the world. You can set up the conditions that will allow MetaValues to prove themselves to you personally. In a sense, each Self-Actualizer has learned to build an individual, mental paraglider that will capture MetaValue energies.

In this book, I will show you how to build yours. I will help you overcome the blocks and fears that have kept you from making the faith-leap into the possibilities of self-actualization. But first you will need to understand the nature of the MetaValue "thermals" that are waiting to lift you out of your present circumstances and carry you to undreamed of happiness and achievement.

Understanding the Power of MetaValues

The "thermals," of course, are the MetaValues themselves. You cannot put MetaValues under a microscope to examine them. You can't weigh or measure Truth, Beauty, and Goodness in physical terms. Much like thermals, we know MetaValues exist because we can take note of how they influence the behavior of observable, finite things. As I explained in the Introduction, the MetaValue terms of Integrity, Excellence, and Caring are not to be substituted for the classic values; they are, rather, expressions of the MetaValues of Truth, Beauty, and Goodness *made visible through action.*

Most people have been conditioned to believe that values are purely humanly-contrived ideas, a kind of furniture for the mind. When Abraham Maslow announced that he had discovered MetaValues operating as *active agents* influencing the behavior of every self-actualizing person he studied, his colleagues were shocked. Maslow wrote, "[MetaValues] are perceived, not invented … They exist beyond the life of the individual. They can be conceived to be a kind of perfection. They could conceivably satisfy the human longing for certainty." [14]

Maslow's ideas about values are probably very far from what you may have read or heard. The common claim is, "My values are mine and yours are yours." This can be accurate enough when applied to our tastes for things such as clothing, music, and food, but it is not valid at all when applied to the cardinal issues of Truth and Integrity. You may have come to believe that values are merely admonitions designed by society to keep you in line—various do's and don'ts that operate as reins to hold you back and channel your behavior. Dr. Maslow acknowledged the nature of these society-contrived values, and he determined that they tend to be imposed from the outside. However, as we mature into Self-Actualizers, we begin to resist these intrusive, coerced values. MetaValues then awaken from somewhere inside and begin to stir into action. Unlike the values of childhood that sometimes served as reins to retard and control us, MetaValues are more like a team of powerful horses that pull us along toward uncharted possibilities.

The Secret of Unlocking the Power of MetaValues

There is a secret to unlocking the potential of MetaValues and becoming a Self-Actualizer. Again, this secret has been hiding in plain sight for decades—available to anyone who carefully examines the work of Abraham Maslow. It comes in three parts.

Early on, Dr. Maslow uncovered three attitudes that are unique to Self-Actualizers and potential Self-Actualizers. When he began his studies, Maslow accepted the conventional wisdom that it is natural for most people in our culture to feel unwarranted guilt, crippling shame, and stressful anxiety. As he studied Self-Actualizers, though, he detected that they were relatively free of this baggage. Over time, they developed an attitude of impregnable self-respect. This self-respect was not overbearing or narcissistic, but rather balanced by an equal degree of respect for other people.

How does such extraordinary self-respect evolve? Self-Actualizers are able to endure challenges to their self-worth because they believe that there is a higher, more effective version of themselves to actualize—a more fully developed model. Self-Actualizers sense, in a matter-of-fact way, that there is greatness within them. Most of us share an intuitive belief that we have a higher, better self within. However, the majority of us feel we can't access this self. We believe that, if there was a time when we could have become the best versions of ourselves, that time has passed. We beat ourselves up for our failures. We exaggerate the losses and minimize the wins. We accept that we have limitations. In doing so, we lose the self-respect necessary to release our inner power. The first part of the secret, then, is to restore the natural, innocent self-respect we had as children while also increasing to an equal degree the respect we have for other people.

The second part of the secret is a precious attitude that Maslow uncovered in Self-Actualizers: they assume a nonnegotiable responsibility for the inner life experience. Again, most of us don't have this attitude. For instance, how often do you say things like, "He makes me angry"? How often do you hold resentments about past injustices? How often do you rehash them? What Maslow saw in Self-Actualizers is that they refused to see themselves as victims, regardless of their circumstances. They perceived their lives as their own and understood that, while they did not have absolute control of their fates, they had absolute control over how they *felt* about their fates. They understood that we cannot control what others may do or say—but we have *total* control over our attitudes and responses.

The third part of the secret is that Self-Actualizers habitually make growth decisions rather than safety decisions. Most people live mundane lives that are virtually devoid of courageous decisions; we want structure and predictability. Many individuals with high IQs waste their lives arranging, classifying, and polishing the known rather than enjoying the adventure of discovering the unknown. Yet actualization is all about new and unfolding possibilities. Potential Actualizers are better able to take advantage of these opportunities because they make growth decisions and act on those decisions. Actualizers acquire an independent spirit and a habit of being active, deciding agents rather than tentative, helpless whiners.

No special training is necessary to utilize this secret. You have, right now, access to exactly the same core of power, energy, and inspiration that sustains the top one percent of achievers. But you cannot think your way into the self-actualizing process—you need to act your way into it. You need to make the components of this secret a fundamental part of your everyday life.

With this in mind, let's look at each of the MetaValues.

Truth: The MetaValue Expressed by Uncompromising Integrity

All normal people share a common need to trust the information someone shares with them. This need transcends cultures, languages, and continents. It does not matter whether you are a Harvard professor, a dockworker, or an Australian bushman. We all value the truth and abhor deceit. We cannot imagine rational people who would hold the belief that truth is not important to them.

The MetaValue of Truth is essential to an actualizing personality. When we are accurate in what we say, and do what we promise to do—we express integrity. However, on the deepest level, integrity also means that our talk—especially our inner talk—must honor who we really are. Downplaying ourselves is not noble; it shows a lack of integrity. We must know ourselves and be true to what we really are by striving to become what we ought to be.

How does this depth of integrity relate to the process of self-actualization—to a lifestyle that is constantly moving from what we are toward becoming what we ought to be? Simply put, Self-Actualizers are more real. Maslow referred to the highest values as "Being values" for good reason. He meant that as we actualize more and more of our potentials, we become more and more real.

The term "being" is important to understand, but it is elusive and hard to define. Saint Augustine had a brilliant way of helping us understand its meaning. He showed us that it is the difference between what *has* value and what value *is*. He would ask students, "Would you rather have a beautiful pearl or a mouse?" The answer was always the same, of course, because we would all rather have the valuable pearl than the mouse. Then he would ask, "Would you rather *be* a beautiful pearl or a mouse?" The answer changed at that point. A mouse, limited as it is, has more being, more power to act than a lifeless pearl. Absolute nonbeing is OK for a pearl. But for a human being, it is an unthinkable disaster.

Integrity as a MetaValue requires that we are willing to face and accept the reality of the way we are at a given moment. It would be wrong, however, to say that Self-Actualizers are self-satisfied. They feel reasonable guilt about improvable shortcomings such as laziness, loss of temper, and hurting others. In general, the Self-Actualizer is disturbed by personal discrepancies between what is and what ought to be. Integrity also implies that we are willing to have faith in the possibilities of the vision of what we ought to be and willing to engage in the process of becoming all that we can be.

This MetaValue is not static. It is a living, evolving thing. Integrity involves a constant, tireless effort to integrate what we are with the possibilities of what we ought to be. The ultimate questions we should ask ourselves are not simply, "Who am I?" but also, "What am I becoming?" and "How can I do better?"

We all share a natural, positive response to the MetaValue of Truth. We respond to Truth because we also share, to some degree, an inner endowment that you might call a reality-response. This means we don't have to be helpless victims of the opinions of so-called experts. As laypersons, we have access within to a resource of uncommon sense. We can demonstrate our own inner reality-response to what we recognize as Integrity. Dr. Maslow observed that Self-Actualizers are very much in touch with, and trust in, the authenticity of their inner feelings. They reasonably consider expert opinions, but they are not intimidated or overwhelmed by them.

Individuals who can balance a childlike clarity to perceive and accept the emerging realities of life with a tireless passion to make things better, are released from the fetters of stress, guilt, shame, and mediocrity. Such a remarkable reaction to Truth fosters Integrity and illuminates a closely related source of energy and inspiration for self-empowerment—the MetaValue of Beauty. Love of Truth leads to love of Beauty. For most of us, Beauty is something we enjoy. But enjoyment of Beauty, important as it is, is passive. Actualizers eventually see the need for more beautiful things and strive to make things better by creating more Beauty.

Beauty: the MetaValue of World-Class Excellence

We know people love Beauty when they demonstrate higher and higher levels of order and personal Excellence in their lives. Absolutely nothing will affect your material success to a more important degree than a dedication to—and a love of—Excellence.

How do we determine what is truly excellent? Do we follow the advice of experts? Not slavishly. Maslow warns us that we should avoid the dangers of rule by experts. We should weigh their opinions, but ultimately rely more fully upon our own reality-response. While the experts may argue about the merits of a painting, a book, or a piece of music, we all admire obvious quality in performance. We do not need an expert to tell us when these things please us. Beyond that, we all sense the beauty of excellent service by a waitperson, a salesclerk, or a plumber. We don't need a master chef to tell us we had an excellent meal or a sportswriter to tell us when a basketball player has just made an astounding shot. We recognize Excellence when an impoverished mother raises wonderful children on her own.

Maslow discovered an unmistakable originality, preciseness, and grace in the performance of Self-Actualizers. This remarkable degree of excellence seems to spring naturally from an inner life driven to develop and grow in character. The Actualizer does not strive to acquire things from the environment in the conventional sense, but rather to achieve excellence and increasing perfection in the expression of self. This drive manifests in an unconscious, childlike way.

We need both facts and values. A left-brained scientist will emphasize fact. A right-brained visionary will accentuate values. Both perspectives of reality are necessary to fully recognize Beauty;

they complement each other. Leon Lederman, a Nobel Prize–winning physicist, offers a clue to this relationship in his book, *The God Particle.* He says that the universe is the answer—but what is the question? This brilliant and amusing philosopher-scientist saw the role of modern science as that of discovering something that you may find surprising:

> *"When Coleridge tried to define beauty, he returned always to one deep thought: beauty, he said, is 'unity in variety.' Science is nothing else than the search to discover unity in the wild variety of nature—or more exactly, in the variety of our experience."* [15]

We see beauty when we detect a harmonious unity of colors and patterns in nature and art. We also hear beauty as music in the melodious arrangement of notes. We enjoy the beauty of words masterfully unified in prose and poetry. We experience beauty in textures, smell it in lovely fragrances, and even taste it. Beyond the physical senses, we discern beauty intellectually in ideas, in what Shakespeare called the mind's eye. Thus, beauty is unity in variety for not only the scientist, but also the visionary, the religionist, the artist, and the poet. On one level, we may debate about what is beautiful. But on another, we generally share a favorable reality-response to unity in variety.

Self-Actualizers are driven to create beauty. It is a turning point when Actualizers realize they have a role—actually a mission—to create something true, beautiful, and good where it did not exist before; something that is excellent, greater than self, and worth any sacrifice. Self-Actualizers feel called, much in the manner that members of the clergy feel themselves called.

The life missions chosen by Actualizers are unselfish duties that benefit humankind in general. The passion and energy focused upon these missions are extraordinary.

There is an interesting side effect of the Actualizer's commitment to a mission they believe has supreme importance. This person is aware of the evil and chaos in the world, but is less acutely disturbed by it than most people are. Actualizers are doing all they can within their spheres of influence. Therefore, they are not wringing their hands; they are taking action, attempting to make things better.

While Self-Actualizers trust their inner feelings and are remarkably independent, they also know that they cannot be a law unto themselves. This brings us to the third MetaValue, which is necessary to avoid the fatal landmine of narcissism. Integrity and Excellence help illuminate this third dimension of reality-response that all Self-Actualizers share—Goodness or Caring. It is perhaps the most important MetaValue of all. It is also the most challenging, because one cannot practice it in a vacuum. Goodness involves the development of caring and respectful relationships with other people.

Goodness: The MetaValue of Caring

Goodness is vastly more than a technique for being nice and getting along with other people. Goodness fosters the quality of Caring in a self-actualizing personality. Goodness modifies the drive to excel, resulting in a wholesome tension between self-interest and service to others. Without Caring and respect for all human life, any political, industrial, or religious philosophy or movement eventually corrupts into a lethal danger to humankind.

Self-Actualizers share a definite tendency to see the life experience as a wonderful gift. To most people, existence becomes stale as we grow older; dimness sets in. But to Self-Actualizers, life becomes new again. There is rebirth, the "second naiveté." Today's sunset once more appears as beautiful and fresh as the first sunset they ever noticed with awe and appreciation. A flower examined today appears full of wonder and beauty, even though they've seen a million flowers before. The thousandth baby seems as miraculous as the first. And this ever-fresh appreciation eventually extends to personal relationships. Self-Actualizers may consider themselves as lucky after thirty-five years of marriage as they did on their wedding days.

As sunshine and water nurture a tree, MetaValues nurture the Self-Actualizer. For some Self-Actualizers, their quest for Goodness and Beauty is inspired and fueled by nature. Others find joy by observing and relating to children. Many draw strength and inspiration from great music.

Maslow noted that all Self-Actualizers derive great pleasure from the day-to-day process of life itself—yet none of his subjects got much out of things like partying or receiving a windfall of money. This is not to suggest that that they are staid or boring people. Many Self-Actualizers derive inspiration from deep and even lusty love relationships. Where they differentiate themselves from ordinary people is in their ability to count their blessings. The lack of this ability among most of us is a common generator of suffering, pain, regret, and loss of self-respect. Husbands, wives, parents, and children are too often appreciated more after they have died than when they are still alive and able to enjoy the attention. Likewise, we tend to value good health, freedom, and economic well-being much more highly when they are lost.

Self-Actualizers assume the role of a loving and patient big brother or big sister. Self-Actualizers do things better than most people they know, accomplish more, and appear to be relatively fearless in the face of the immensity of destiny. They are also independent, and may often appear withdrawn and aloof. Yet, in spite of occasional feelings of annoyance at the weaknesses of others, Self-Actualizers have a genuine desire to help the human race. However isolated Actualizers may feel from their fellow creatures at times, they retain a kinship toward humanity in general. "It is as if they were all members of a single family," Maslow noted. "One's feelings toward his brothers would be on the whole affectionate, even if these brothers were foolish, weak, or even if they were sometimes nasty." [16]

Self-Actualizers are also color-, status-, and class-blind in their relationships. They are friendly and open with any person of suitable character. They are willing to learn from anyone who is willing to teach them. In the role of a learner, Actualizers demonstrate what can only be called humility. They exhibit no pretenses or attempts to retain dignity or status of any kind. They have an authentic respect for anyone who demonstrates unusual skill and knowledge in a particular field.

Still, Self-Actualizers are discriminating in their choice of associates. They choose from the elite, but it is an elite of character, capacity, and talent rather than worldly status or rank. They choose their close relationships carefully, usually people who are further along in the process of self-actualization than the average. This, of course, limits their pool of friends because there are so few who have reached these levels.

Self-Actualizers do not find funny what most people call humor. They do not enjoy racial slurs or hostile humor (making people laugh by poking fun at someone), superiority humor (laughing at someone's perceived inferiority), or smutty, potty humor. They are philosophical in their humor, often making fun of pretentiousness and self-aggrandizement. A principal characteristic of Self-Actualizers is that they often laugh at themselves, especially their own vanities and shortcomings. The Self-Actualizer is amused by human pride, busyness, ambition, self-absorption, and the like.

Achieving Synergy

When combined with Integrity and Excellence, the MetaValue of Caring exponentially increases charisma and one's power of being. When all three MetaValues are coordinated and made real in personality experience, the result is synergy. Synergy is a term coined by Ruth Benedict to describe what happens when the nature—or power—of a system cannot be predicted by adding up its parts. For example, when you integrate two volatile gases (oxygen and hydrogen), you get water—a liquid that puts out fires. In the same light, when MetaValues are in perfect sync and harmony, Actualizers will often perform far beyond their expected capacity. Synergy is not exclusively science, nor philosophy, nor religion. It is rather an integration of all three.

Synergy takes place when a fine pianist achieves a moment of transcendence, when he is observing himself playing without conscious effort and playing in a magnificent way. There have been many names for synergy over the years. Charles Garfield, an Olympic coach, discovered that athletes reach levels of performance like this and called it *Peak Performance* or being *in the zone*. Psychologist and noted author Mihaly Csikszentmihalyi calls it *Flow*. We will discuss the secrets of these performance pioneers in later chapters.

Dr. Maslow referred to the ultimate human state of consciousness as the *Peak Experience*. His research revealed that most people, whether Actualizers or not, achieved a peak experience state for brief periods. Maslow believed that this state of being happens when all three MetaValues are in perfect balance and fuse into one. This fusion produces Love in its most pure and effective expression. Not romantic love, but love on another level, one that includes all human relationships. He wrote:

> *"I believe that synergy is an actual perception of a higher truth, of a higher reality, which actually exists and that the development over into synergy is like the development from becoming blind into becoming seeing … The truth is that human interests, especially when people know each other and love each other, are pooled rather than being mutually exclusive. Any analysis of good marriage can easily show this. Any analysis of a good partnership in business can easily show this."* [17]

Dr. Maslow believed that it is not too far from saying that one's responsibility to one's life and activities is like a love relationship, a recognition of belongingness, and the need to strive for greater and greater being. Maslow saw this MetaValue fusion of Integrity, Caring, and Excellence into the ultimate MetaValue of Love as an unlimited resource. He believed that in a relationship of

Caring, respect, and appreciation, love breeds more love, and the spending of love does not diminish love, but instead creates a greater wealth of love.

What Does All of This Mean to You?

There's a good chance that your response to the notions of MetaValues and self-actualization is that it is the exclusive domain of superpeople. Certainly, the highest levels of peak performance are available to a limited few. But all of us can embrace and benefit immensely by incorporating MetaValues into our lives.

Remember the three parts of the secret that set the MetaValues process into motion:

> *An impregnable self-respect.*
>
> *A nonnegotiable responsibility for the inner life.*
>
> *A habitual willingness to make growth decisions rather than safety decisions.*

These are the three precious attitudes that unlock the door. And they are readily available to you. All you need to do is set up the conditions that will allow MetaValues to prove themselves to you. You can begin to do so immediately.

It is your unquestionable birthright to confront the day's challenges lifted by the wings of confidence and love. Yet most of us, even the wealthy, wake up every morning believing that life is about the struggle to survive and get ahead in a world of limited resources.

It does not have to be that way. This is what Rosamund Stone Zander and Benjamin Zander said in *The Art of Possibility*.

> *"Let us suppose, now, that a universe of possibility stretches beyond the world of measurement to include all worlds: infinite, generative, and abundant. Unimpeded on a daily basis by the concern for survival, free from the generalized assumption of scarcity, a person stands in the great space of possibility in a posture of openness, with an unfettered imagination for what can be … Emotions that are often regulated to the special category of spirituality are abundant here: joy, grace, awe, wholeness, passion, and compassion."* [18]

One of the primary objectives of this book is to help you achieve your positive recognition and actualization of a completely new universe of possibilities. I have researched, gathered, and tested the material in these pages for decades. I have used every technique or method recommended in this book successfully myself and with other people.

For the first time in history, large numbers of people have the freedom to choose. You are one of them. How can you be sure you will choose correctly? How will you acquire an impregnable self-respect so that you won't run out of gas and give up as you have so many times before? How will you achieve an inner life of sustained peace and power? The answer lies within, with your personal MetaValues breakthrough.

But first, you must remove the blocks that prevent the full activation of that breakthrough.

CHAPTER TWO
The Jonah Complex or the Will-to-Fail

"We fear our highest possibilities (as well as our lowest ones). We are generally afraid to become that which we can glimpse in our most perfect moments, under the most perfect conditions, under conditions of greatest courage. We enjoy and even thrill at the godlike possibilities we see in ourselves in such peak moments. And yet we simultaneously shiver with weakness, awe, and fear before these very same possibilities." [19]

ABRAHAM MASLOW
The Farther Reaches of Human Nature

"… we are victims of a Will to Fail; that unless we see this in time and take action against it we die without accomplishing our intentions … We all live so far below the possible level for our lives that when we are set free from the things that hamper us so that we merely approach the potentialities in ourselves, we seem to have been entirely transfigured. It is in comparison with the halting, tentative, hesitant lives we let ourselves live that the full, normal life that is ours by right seems to partake of the definitely supernormal … But those who … cannot find in religion or philosophy the strength that they need to counteract their own ineffectiveness, can still teach themselves by conscious effort to get the best from their lives." [20]

DOROTHEA BRANDE
Wake Up and Live

A. J. Cronin looked, but his eyes could not pierce the misty Scottish morning. The ferocious mountains and hills of the Highlands where his doctor had banished him loomed dimly; the road that led from his small white cottage disappeared completely after only a dozen feet in the gloomy fog. With a heavy sigh, Cronin turned away from the window and sat down at the simple kitchen table.[21]

At that moment, Cronin thought of himself as a victim. Little did he know at that point that he was undergoing one of those remarkable redirecting cataclysms that change our lives. Most of us have experienced such episodes—hurled out of a comfortable situation into a challenging, difficult predicament that forced us to change. Perhaps we can now say, in retrospect, that the episode was beneficial and we are glad it happened. But amidst the turmoil such a calamity creates, we rarely recognize the "hand of the angel." Instead, we tend to believe that fate has been unkind to us.

In the case of the thirty-three-year-old Cronin, only a couple of weeks before, he had been a medical doctor in London with a very busy and successful West End practice. Most people looked upon him with envy, wishing their lives could be as rich and meaningful as his. Yet, in his heart of hearts, Cronin was dissatisfied. So much so that a gastric ulcer began to eat away at his stomach. The symptoms of chronic indigestion finally forced him to consult a colleague— who demanded he take "six months of total and complete rest in the country on a milk diet."

So it was that Cronin found himself in a tiny farmhouse on Fyne Farm, staring at the top of a crude kitchen table with nothing to do. All his life he had been a busy, driving man—he'd been able to ignore the messages of discontent that his heart sent him. Now he had nothing to divert him. Alone on a chilly Scottish morning, he sensed a force stirring faintly within him. The force would grow considerably stronger in the days to come.

At last, an idea—a vision long nurtured in the higher, superconscious realms of his mind—broke through.

"I will write a novel," Cronin announced to himself.

In the utter stillness of that morning, in a rare interval of openness, Cronin realized that he had wanted to write most of his life. Now the vision of a book emerged effortlessly in his mind; it was clearly defined and inspiring. Cronin could hardly wait for the small store in the nearby village of Talbert to open, so he could buy some writing materials.

The blissful burst of creative energy soon gave way to the arduous process of making that creativity tangible. Cronin had a clear idea that he wanted to write a story about the tragic results of a man's egoism and pride. He even had a title: *Hatter's Castle*. Yet, after returning from the store in the village, he sat for three hours staring frozenly at a blank page in one of the notebooks he had purchased.

Then Cronin recalled the advice of an old schoolmaster. "Get it down!" the man said. "If it stops in your head, it will always be nothing. Get it down." And so he began to *get it down*. The work was slow beyond anything he could have imagined. He had never written anything more profound than prescriptions in "dog Latin." He had no idea of style, form, or technique. He had never seen a thesaurus. The difficulty of creating a single useful sentence bordered on overwhelming. He spent hours seeking an adjective. He spent more hours correcting and re-correcting until some pages became so jumbled and confusing that he tore them up and started over.

Yet Cronin continued and the process of writing began to engulf him. The characters became real; they talked back to him, wept, laughed, and haunted his dreams. In the middle of the night, he was often compelled to answer their call. Sprawled out on the floor, he would obediently express one of their new ideas by dim candlelight. At first, Cronin could produce only 800 words a day. Slowly, he increased this to 2,000 (about eight minutes of fiction reading for the average reader).

The Intrusion of the Will-to-Fail

As unprepared as Cronin was for the arduous process of creating, he was even less ready for the abrupt intrusion of the Jonah Complex—the Will-to-Fail. Halfway through his novel, a silent avalanche of despair swept over him. Cronin began the inner self-abuse that destroys the overwhelming majority of the creative projects of humanity. "Who am I to imagine I could do this?" he declared one morning. "I am not a writer; I am preposterously ill-equipped and untrained. This project will never amount to anything."

In a fever of desperation, Cronin rushed over to his desk to read the first chapter of his book, which had just arrived from London where his secretary had typed it. After doing so, he sank into even deeper dismay and self-scorn. "No one will ever read this tripe! I was a presumptuous lunatic to imagine I could write a novel. All I have written, all I will ever write is futile, wasted effort!" Angry now and embarrassed, Cronin bundled up the entire manuscript, his notebooks, and his papers, and marched outside and dumped them into the trash can. In grim satisfaction, he watched the light rain that was falling begin to soak his project. He knew it would soon dissolve into merciful oblivion.

Cronin put on his jacket and cap and plunged down the road. He walked in the rain a free man. He believed his surrender was prudent; it had liberated him from the torturous ordeal of writing. He sighed in relief, utterly prepared to put this failed episode behind him.

But his decision to walk in the rain was a fateful one. As it turned out, A. J. Cronin was walking *toward* his destiny, not away from it.

"I Canna Help But Dig"

Halfway down the loch shore, Cronin saw the outline of a figure digging in the drizzling rain. It was Old Angus, a farmer who seemingly spent every spare moment digging his small patch of boggy land. Bit by bit, he turned over the wet soil of the bog in an effort to make it arable. As Cronin approached, he could hear the scraping of the shovel and the grunts of the dogged farmer.

Old Angus looked up and greeted Cronin. Angus knew of Cronin's writing project and he silently approved of it. The Scots have a tradition of deep respect and admiration for those who create literature.

"Are ye not writing today?" he asked.

"Oh, no," Cronin replied. "I realized this morning that I am ill-equipped to be a writer. I decided to scuttle the project."

Cronin observed the weathered old face of Old Angus slowly change. His intense blue eyes locked Cronin's in a merciless gaze of disappointed contempt.

Finally, Angus began to speak in a somber voice. "You know, doctor, you are probably the one who is right and I am probably wrong. But, my father ditched this bog all of his days and he never made a pasture out of it. And I have dug in it all of my days and I have not yet made a pasture. But, pasture or no pasture, I canna help but dig. Because my father knew, and I know, that if you will only dig long enough, a pasture can be made here."

He turned slightly away to resume digging, and then looked up and added, "Perhaps it's the same with your wee book."

Cronin felt his face grow hot with anger as Angus then ignored him to continue his digging. Cronin resented this man who had what he did not have—an unflinching stubbornness to see the job through at all costs.

More important, though, he began to recognize in himself a syndrome of the root of all failure: the collapse of the human creative will. His own defeat seemed magnified into a symbol, a symbol of humankind's common tendency to retreat into comfort rather than to make an arduous advance with no assurance of reward.

Cronin turned and tramped back to Fyne Farm. Rain-soaked, humiliated, and angry, Cronin murmured to himself, "At least I shall finish it. By God, at least I shall finish it." He fished the soggy bundle of papers from the trash can and dried it in the kitchen oven.

Three months later, he wrote *"finis"* at the bottom of a page of one of his notebooks and sat back in triumph. He had kept his promise; he had created a novel. It did not matter whether it was good or not. Cronin felt a level of emancipation now that vastly exceeded the freedom of escape he had sought before by quitting. Indeed, he wondered how he could have considered abandoning the project.

Cronin chose a publisher by closing his eyes and sticking a pin in a directory. He then mailed the typed manuscript and forgot it.

In the last month of his exile, his health returned and he felt a strong urge to get back to work. He began to say his final good-byes to the folks around the village. To his surprise, the postmaster of Talbert greeted him with a telegram from the publisher. Cronin immediately took the telegram to Old Angus and showed it to him without a word. Angus simply nodded his approval.

The novel that Cronin had thrown away, *Hatter's Castle*, was to sell millions of copies. It was eventually translated into nineteen languages, dramatized for the stage, and adapted for the screen. Cronin would go on to write many significant novels, among them *The Citadel* and *Keys to the Kingdom*. His life, of course, changed dramatically.

What would have happened had Cronin not chanced to meet Old Angus on that morning of destiny? No doubt *Hatter's Castle* would now be but another of the mass of unfinished projects that have fallen victim to the Will-to-Fail.

And what of our own abandoned plans and unfinished projects? What if we had met an Old Angus at the critical moment of their abandonment?

The Great Destroyer: The Jonah Complex

Jonah was an Old Testament prophet who sought to avoid his destiny. God had commanded him to evangelize in a particularly evil city and Jonah tried to stay away from this task by taking a sea voyage. In the end, his destiny caught up with him and he yielded to God's will.

To demonstrate how the Jonah Complex destroys creative expression, Abraham Maslow created an allegory about a college student who decides to rewrite Plato in modern language. The student begins with a great passion for the project, dedicates himself to it, and then pulls up short. At some point in the enterprise, the student is assaulted by immense misgivings. He sees himself as unworthy, the task as grandiose and futile. Plato shines as some majestic icon and he is but a pathetic student working under a dim lamp on a beat-up table in a lonely dorm. He ridicules his efforts, abandons the undertaking, and accepts defeat. However, Dr. Maslow suggests that it was entirely possible that Plato himself had similar misgivings at times. Plato, though, did not quit.

Why do most of us fail to fulfill our ambitions? What paralyzes the will-to-achieve? Why are closets and attics all over America cluttered with half-finished projects? Why do about ninety percent of our potentials lie fallow and unused? Why do most of us work so hard to avoid our destinies?

To some degree, we falter because of the power of the opinions of others to affect our actions. Abraham Maslow referred to the tendency of humanity to ridicule and denigrate the noble efforts of others as "countervaluing." Encouragement, appreciation, and respect—such as Old Angus gave to A. J. Cronin—cost nothing, and yet we have made them among the rarest and most wanted commodities on earth. We have all been victims of countervaluing; we have all inflicted its destructive force upon others.

One reason people tend to be negative about the worthy efforts of others is that they are often intimidated by the MetaValues those efforts represent. We do not want a friend to achieve anything that would expose, by contrast, our own failures. We don't even want our best friend to go on a successful diet if we know we need to go on a diet also. We do not want to see a companion forsake the comfort of the status quo and risk living at another level if we remain cringing inside our comfort zones.

Most often, though, we inflict the negativity of countervaluing upon ourselves. One example of self-inflicted countervaluing is what I call the Jonah Compromise. An example of this would be an intelligent, gifted person dumbing down to try to fit in with the crowd. Potential Actualizers might have strong impulses to express themselves, only to find themselves punished by their peers and authority figures for being different and outstanding. Therefore, most of us compromise to avoid the counter-hostility we fear. In doing so, we repress the inner desire to express ourselves.

However, the inner self will not be still. Those noble dreams and awesome potentials soon seek expression. Conflicts and difficulties arise. For most of us, this results in a kind of inner shame and self-depreciation. Few are strong enough to challenge the polite deceit that permeates typical social intercourse.

We then rationalize that our aspirations were not so important anyway. Why leave the comfortable sanctuary of the known to chance an obscure fate? Why risk everything we have gained with no assurance of victory if we take a new path, especially without even a clear vision of what it is we are seeking?

The answer is that just beyond our greatest fear lies peace and freedom. And, too often, we give up the struggle and stand like helpless lost children when we are barely inches from home.

The Rare Ability to Go the Distance

A. J. Cronin's story is inspiring, but it is much more. It reflects a principle to hold high: *When in doubt, go the distance.*

At some point in life, the Will-to-Fail syndrome takes hold; most people unconsciously commence the avoidance process. They delay, and then give up their dreams. You have seen this, or will see it, in most of your friends. One by one, they will drop away from the bitter struggle of life and begin to go through the motions.

Only rarely does a human continue to get up after being knocked down repeatedly by life. Most of us eventually decide to stay down to avoid the pain of falling again. We become what is known in sports as a game loser, someone who struggles bravely but never quite puts up enough fight to win. But when we make a final and irrevocable decision to get up again no matter what—to go the distance regardless of how many times we are knocked down—something happens. Things begin to change. Invisible forces come to our aid. We are on the side of life.

Breaking the Sonic Crystal Wall

The Jonah Complex is aided by another factor: the Chaos Syndrome. When we are inches from success, chaos seems to rain down on us.

Everything seems to be going to pieces. It feels like any moment we will hit the wall. Legendary test pilot Chuck Yeager faced this problem in a vivid, literal way.

Back in 1947, Chuck Yeager climbed into his Bell X-1 jet plane with uncompromising determination. Yeager wanted to do what no one had ever done before: he wanted to break the sonic barrier. Back then, some scientists believed that the barrier was like a solid wall that would destroy any plane that attempted to go faster than sound. In truth, planes take a tremendous buffeting at near-sonic speed due to the formation of shock waves. Some planes had actually shattered in an attempt to reach supersonic speeds and there was strong belief that these speeds would cause the human body irreparable harm.

Yeager soared high over the desert and began to open the throttle of his Bell X-1. As he passed the 700-mile-per-hour mark, the plane began to shudder. Still, with fifty miles per hour to go before he reached the supersonic barrier, Yeager kept the throttle down. The plane began to shake violently. The glass in the instrument panel shattered. Yeager could barely keep a grip on the joystick because it was vibrating with such fury. Any minute the plane could fall apart. Then, with one final immense shudder, the Bell X-1 passed the sonic barrier and a great stillness came over the craft. Yeager felt the smoothness and awesome power of his jet as he soared across the trackless sky. The sonic barrier was not a barrier at all. The dangers it posed came exclusively from design problems.

The MetaValues Breakthrough professes that there is a crystal wall of human limitations much like the sound barrier. This barrier is one generated by the creative imagination. In this case, it is a software design problem. We are programmed to fear impending doom when we exceed our comfort zones. In virtually every human project, there is a moment of chaos that causes most people to flinch and give up. We need an exquisite self-respect to surmount these.

Should You Ever Give Up?

Winston Churchill is often quoted as saying: "Never give in, never give in, never, never, never, never give in ..." Most people who quote him, however, tend to leave out the second part of his sentence, in which he said, "except to convictions of honor or good sense." There is a time to give up on an ill-advised project, but how can we know when that time comes? Some people continue to struggle with a project that has long lost any chance of success only because they have already put so much into it.

This is the counter-principle to the Jonah Complex—the *Previous Investment Trap.* Only the individuals involved can make the call, but generally, a decision to continue with a project or a relationship should never be based upon how much you have already invested in it. There is a time to cut bait and sail on. This is not to suggest that it is ever advisable to abandon a project in a mood of fear, laziness, discouragement, or self-depreciation. Such a decision should be objective, a prudent weighing of realities, costs, and potential benefits.

And, as always, when in doubt, go the distance.

The Safety vs. Growth Conundrum

Imagine a wooden beam that is only six inches wide lying on the floor in front of you. If you were asked to walk the length of the beam, you could do so without difficulty. Yet, if the same beam were raised up a thousand feet and placed between two buildings, you would probably refuse to even try to walk it. Why? Because a vision of failure would flash before you; you would see yourself falling and fear would immobilize you.

Now imagine a snarling, savagely hungry bear just behind you. The thought of being killed by the bear flashes before you. Suddenly you are willing to attempt to cross the chasm. Your vision of certain death overpowers your vision of possible death.

Suppose now that there is no bear, but you are ravenously hungry. Across the chasm is food. Again, you would risk crossing the beam because you would be compelled to do that rather than face impending death by starvation.

Finally, imagine that by crossing the chasm, all of your hopes and dreams would be fulfilled. Would you cross? The problem becomes less tangible, and more difficult to address. Any thinking person would hesitate and consider the risk relative to the gain. In this case, unfortunately, a safety need usually overpowers a higher motivation. This is why we tend to make safety decisions in preference to growth decisions. We prefer, like Hamlet, to surrender to those "ills we have" than to "fly to others that we know not of."

And yet, if you believed the prizes you sought were positively on the other side of the chasm, and if you had faith that you could walk the beam without falling, then nothing short of some cosmic or moral duty could interfere with your commitment to attempt the crossing.

Day by day, almost moment by moment, we face a version of this choice: safety or growth? Should we be cautious and stay with the known and the relatively comfortable, or should we risk?

Mihaly Csikszentmihalyi, a noted expert in the psychology of enlightened consciousness, expresses it this way:

> *"The best moments usually occur when a person's body or mind is stretched to its limits in a voluntary effort to accomplish something difficult and worthwhile. Optimal experience is thus something that we make happen. For a child, it could be placing with trembling fingers the last block on a tower she has built, higher than any she has built so far; for a swimmer, it could be trying to beat his own record; for a violinist, mastering an intricate musical passage. For each person there are thousands of opportunities, challenges to expand ourselves."* [22]

As you accept your own growth challenges, realize that failure or success are equally products of creative imagination. Failure is a conspiracy of the two hemispheres of the brain. One hemisphere, the conceptual side of the brain, "sees" failure, while the other, the logical, cautious side, accepts the vision and shuts down. The will freezes. The conceptual side of the human brain is the physical seat of creative imagination. Recall that Cronin first "saw" a completed novel. The more vivid and fear-charged vision of failing and being ridiculed temporarily obscured this vision. The vision of failure was, in turn, dispelled when he was subjected to derisive scorn for abandoning the project.

Our creative imaginations can help us achieve wonderful things, or they can be used to torture us and fill us with fear. Our human destiny largely hinges upon whether we use the gift of human creative imagination wisely and constructively, or whether we become victims of the phantoms of our own creation. In essence, every battle is won or lost before it is fought.

Who's Afraid of the Manassas Mauler?

During the Roaring Twenties, Jack Dempsey was the heavyweight boxing champion of the world. He was considered virtually invincible. Called the Manassas Mauler after his hometown in Colorado, he fought with ferocious energy, intimidating and defeating all opposition. Along came a challenger named Gene Tunney. Tunney was a scientific boxer who had studied films of Dempsey's fights for years. Tunney determined that Dempsey had a weakness that he believed he could exploit and use to defeat the champion. Dempsey had a devastating left hook. However, Tunney noted that just before Dempsey threw the left hook he lowered his left hand slightly, exposing his own jaw. Tunney became convinced that in that split second of exposure he could throw his own right and beat the champion to the punch. Repeatedly, Tunney visualized the right hand counterpunch in his mind. Finally, Tunney got his opportunity to fight Dempsey and he was positive he could win.

But a month before the fight, he made a serious mistake. He began reading the sports pages of six major newspapers. Almost no one believed Tunney had a chance. All the leading sportswriters picked Dempsey by a knockout.

Pictures began to form in Tunney's imagination—new pictures of defeat. He began to have nightmares. He dreamed he was lying beaten on the canvas with Dempsey poised nearby ready to finish him off if he got up. One night, he awoke and felt his bed shaking. He could not imagine what was happening. Then he realized he himself was shaking in fear. Terror overwhelmed him. Later he told the story of how he dealt with the Will-to-Fail:

> *"I couldn't stop trembling. Right there, I had already lost the ring match, which meant everything to me— the championship. I had lost it—unless I could regain it. I got up and took stock of myself. What could I do about the terror? I could guess the cause. I had been thinking about the fight in the wrong way. I had been reading the newspapers, and all they had said was how Tunney would lose. Through the newspapers I was losing the battle in my own mind ... When the nightmares persisted, despite my inner conviction that I knew how to beat Dempsey, and indeed would, I decided to stop reading the sports pages, and did until after the fight. I simply had to close the doors of my mind to the destructive thoughts and divert my attention to other things."* [23]

Tunney's favorite pastime was reading. After training, instead of reading the sports pages, he began to read Shakespeare and his favorite classic literature. Even on the day of the big contest, he read and relaxed. On September 23, 1926, more than 145,000 fans jammed Sesquicentennial Stadium in Philadelphia for the historic event. A calm Gene Tunney awaited the mighty Manassas Mauler. When Dempsey stepped into the ring, Tunney got up from his stool and walked over to greet him. "Hello, champion," he said. Somewhat surprised, Dempsey replied, "Hello, Gene." When the bell rang, however, Dempsey was all business and began stalking the challenger. Shortly into the first round, Dempsey lowered his left hand in preparation for throwing his deadly hook. Instantly, just as he had mentally rehearsed it, Tunney unleashed a powerful right. The punch landed flush on Dempsey's cheek and jarred him down to his toes. He was stopped in his tracks. Tunney said later that he believed the fight was practically over the second he landed that powerful right hand:

> *"That blow won the fight. Dempsey was dazed for the rest of the battle, and I was a certainty to outpoint him for the championship. Jack was battered and worn out at the end, and I may have knocked him out if the bout went a few rounds more."* [24]

The lesson is clear. We are often victims of the Will-to-Fail because we believe things that someone else simply makes up. We fail when we rehearse failure and succeed when we rehearse success. Stories such as Gene Tunney's, Chuck Yeager's, and A. J. Cronin's are valuable. Children who are told positive, inspiring stories—and told them regularly and personally by someone they respect and trust—prove to be far more motivated.

But where does the seemingly invincible confidence of a Chuck Yeager come from? How was Gene Tunney able to snatch victory from the jaws of certain defeat? How does one develop such character and confidence? It all begins with an impregnable self-respect. And the surprising secret of such sublime self-respect is that we can only respect ourselves to the degree we respect other people. We will explore this next.

TAKING ACTION

Stories inspire, but action is everything. It is important—critically important—that you begin to put the information you read on these pages into action immediately. Our most powerful defense against the Will-to-Fail is an impregnable self-respect. But until we learn more about how to develop such confidence, we may need a tactical gimmick or two in the interim.

Write your own headlines. Other people have been writing your headlines for you. Just as the sports writers underestimated Gene Tunney, so your friends and associates underestimate you. Quit reading their headlines and begin to write your own. Don't just think them; put them on paper every day. There is significant power in writing down your own headlines. Each morning, go over the challenges that confront you. Probably there are three, four, or five specific issues that intimidate you to some degree. Compose a series of headlines reporting today's successful accomplishments-to-be. Keep them close at hand. Read them during the day.

Form a vivid vision of success and cling to it. Remember how Tunney clearly pictured his pivotal blow that changed the course of his fight with Jack Dempsey. Create your own outrageously confident and daring visual of success. At the end of the day, do an action review—check the headlines you anticipated and weigh them against your actual accomplishments.

CHAPTER THREE
An Impregnable Self-Respect

"The healthy individual, because he has great respect for himself, is able to be more respectful to others. This is supported by Erich Fromm's contention that true … self-respect is harmonious with, rather than antagonistic to, love for others. The average individual, lacking sufficient self-respect, does not form deep respectful relationships with others." [25]

> *FRANK G. GOBLE*
> *The Third Force*

"The first thing we are going to do in here children, … is an awful lot of believing in ourselves …

"I love you, I love you all, and I am going to continue to love you and care about you and worry about you … If you stop learning, if you stop building your minds, then everything I have been teaching you is wasted." [26]

> *MARVA COLLINS*
> *Marva Collins' Way*

Since the new school had only four pupils, a fresh student was, at first, a welcome sight. But as Marva Collins invited the child in, her heart began to sink. Erika McCoy was a chubby six years of age. She seemed disoriented and confused. The child moved as one severely disturbed—deliberately walking into the wall, then into desks, finally knocking over a chair. The other children burst into laughter. With a few uncharacteristically brusque words, Marva silenced the other children.

Marva tried to ignore the now-stifled laughter. Erika had evidently been dressed to look pretty, with a nice velveteen jumper, white knee socks, and patent leather shoes. But her general appearance was one of dishevelment; one sock hung down, her feet were half out of her shoes as she broke the backs with her heels, one ribbon was untied, and she was chewing on the other.

Like her new classmates, Erika was a reject. Erika had been dismissed from a Lutheran parochial school. Her teacher had declared, "Erika cannot read and probably will never be able to read. She needs to be in a special class." Yet, the children Erika began to observe in this classroom were not behaving like rejects. She watched and listened as Marva Collins led them through their arithmetic lesson, weaving in snippets of history, geography, English, and even a few words of French as she interacted with the active young minds.

"I Hug Them Until Their Eyes Begin to Dance"

Marva Collins was a remarkably gifted African American teacher. She was convinced that without self-respect the human mind cannot function properly, because the will is incapacitated. She founded her little private school and ran it differently than the stilted '70s Chicago school system she had left in dismay. Marva went to virtually any length to restore the destroyed self-respect of each "problem child" that enrolled in her school. "I hug them until their eyes begin to dance, and then I begin to teach," she once said of her system.

Later, Marva would gain notoriety and her children would perform superlatively in national academic tests. She had a gift that kindled fire in the minds of her students and transformed them into scholars. Someone once said, "Formal education is to learning what a guided tour is to adventure," but that statement did not apply to the classes of Marva Collins. Her students were educated beyond the confines of math, English, and cold history, into the realms of literature and art. When national television broadcast her story and showed her classes, viewers watched in awe as little children quoted Shakespeare and Chaucer with ease, and confidently defined words that might stump a college student.

Marva Collins used a teaching system that was student-driven. For years, education analysts have attempted to formulate various approaches to learning based upon student personality types and standardized needs. For Marva, there were no types, there was only the single individual child before her. By deeply respecting, observing, and listening to her pupils, the unique needs of each child eventually emerged. Marva Collins held high principles and values as an ideal standard, yet she tailored her expertise and teaching skills to each individual student. In the case of Erika, she confronted a formidable new challenge. Marva Collins loved her children without condition, but wise and energetic love is not static, it must be redefined in each emerging reality situation.

Unlike other students, Erika did not seem to respond to the kindness, love, and assurance that Marva lavished upon her. "She's crazy," one of the students would say—and although Marva would silence such remarks, deep down she became confused. After two months, Erika's behavior was as disturbing as it had been on the first day. In the middle of a lesson, Erika might leave her seat, sit on the floor, and begin to scoot around. She took her socks off and chewed them; wrote with crayon all over her reader; and rubbed against the chalkboard, covering herself with dust. Her mother reported that Erika would grab the steering wheel of the car while she drove and that, in traffic, Erika once threw a sweater over her mother's head.

One lunchtime, Erika took the cap off her thermos and let juice dribble all over her dress. She took apart her sandwich and began licking the bread, getting mayonnaise all over her face. The other children began to giggle. Suddenly, she looked at the group and declared: "My teacher said I can't read." Marva, ready to burst into tears, said: "If you don't forget what that teacher told you, I'm going to get terribly angry!" The enemy was clearly defined for Marva, the familiar foe she had hated and defeated before. Here was the malady, not one of a race, but of all humankind: self-defeating limitation.

Programmed to Fail

There is a programming that is pounded into nearly every tiny human mind from the beginnings of consciousness: "You can't." And thus great things are left—not simply undone, but unattempted. And the tragedy is not that the masses of able humanity live self-indulgent lives. The tragedy is that the lives of most people are pathetically innocuous. "You can't" is a powerful trigger that activates the Jonah Complex. Most of humankind has been programmed to believe this lie, and before they have had a chance to live, they have designed a permanent personal epithet: "I can't."

Weeks of effort lay ahead, as Marva sought to undo the programming that had distorted and stupefied a mind that was perhaps more sensitive than most. Tirelessly, the repetitive words of Marva Collins were poured into those little ears: "You are not a bad girl, you are not a stupid child." Yet, there was no discernable change. And one day, just after the Christmas holiday, Erika suddenly jumped up and ran out of the classroom, down the stairs, and out of the building into the frigid Chicago air. Marva chased her down, held her tight, and told Erika that she could not permit her to behave in this way. Erika pushed her away roughly and shouted: "I can do what I want! My mommy lets me! She lets me do what I want!"

At that point, the dismaying mosaic of Erika's behavior took on a simple, identifiable pattern. Marva recalled Erika's mother's indulgences, how she took Erika everywhere she wanted and did everything she demanded. No wonder Marva's generous praise and kindnesses did not work. The child heard such reassurances many times, indulgently and without discrimination. Now Marva saw that Erika had been begging not for attention, but for discipline.

Marva's mind buzzed with this new insight as she took Erika back into the building. She sat the child down at her desk and resumed passing out reading comprehension worksheets mimeographed from the California Achievement Tests. Although Marva didn't have much regard for these tests, she knew her students would need to be proficient at test-taking to succeed in the rest of the academic world. "I don't need any tests to show me how much you know. I see it every day. But we learn to take tests because we live in a world that often judges us by how well we perform on tests."

After coming in from the street, Erika began to tear her test into shreds. The other children watched her closely and Marva said: "Oh, they pay a lot of money to people who tear up paper. You'll get the best job in the world if you learn how to do that, won't you?" The other children shook their heads no. Marva gave Erika a new paper, and told her to circle the synonyms, as she had been told before. "I won't!" Erika screamed.

Marva felt the eyes of the other children on her. She had an intuition that if she did not act decisively, she would lose them all. She whirled around, and seeing a pipe from a vacuum cleaner that the maintenance crew had left, she picked it up and turned, standing over Erika. Staring her dead in the eye, Marva shouted: "If you don't finish your paper I am going to …" The words had scarcely left her lips when Marva felt her own shock that she was threatening Erika. She heard one of the other children gasp and noted they were all staring at her in disbelief. Marva knew, as did Erika on some level, that they had reached a turning point.

Marva had never before threatened a child. In her entire life she had never struck a child, even one of her own. As she trembled with rage, she began to wish that she could drop the pipe and go on with the lesson. She wanted to forget the terrible moment ever happened. But she sensed that she must hold her ground. If Erika called her bluff, all would be lost. So she spoke again to Erika. "Everyone says you are crazy. I don't believe that. But if you don't finish that paper, then I know you are crazy. You might as well be dead as to go through life the way you are."

Erika stared down at the paper, her hands pressed flat against the top of the desk. Her right hand trembled and made a slight movement, touching her pencil. The paper fell off her desk. She bent over slowly and picked it up. Then, with excruciating deliberation, Erika circled the word "throw" as the synonym for "pitch." She moved on to the second question, circling "silly" for "foolish." Marva wanted to laugh for joy. The child had been listening all along! Through all of the tantrums and nonsense, she had been learning. Marva stood there in silence as Erika continued, finally finishing the page. Erika looked up at Marva. "Am I in the first grade or was I put back?" Marva answered: "We don't go backward in here. What is past is past. We only move forward."

The turning point had been reached. Erika became a new child. Yet, it was not, as it may have seemed, a sudden transformation. It was a moment of epiphany that every teacher treasures, when the months of loving attention, the words of encouragement and love, the genuine caring bear fruit. Erika had been testing Marva Collins. Marva knew that the "threat" she made was not the deciding factor. It was Marva's own loyalty that had turned the tide. Marva loyally acted out all her words of reassurance and love; she walked her talk and demonstrated her trustworthiness, her genuine acceptance and respect of Erika. Marva was there for her. Marva wrote, regarding the incident:

> *"After a while Erika's seeming lack of interest was replaced by active curiosity, her lethargy turned into ambition, and her obstreperousness gave way to a measure of self-control. The potential had always been there. It exists in all children. The challenge for a teacher is to bring the potential out. There is no such thing as THE way to reach a student. Any way is THE way as long as it works for the individual child."* [27]

Erika acquired what seemed to be a new persona. Yet, in truth, she had always wanted to please, to be what was expected of her. Marva had established what seemed extravagant expectations—and now Erika was rising to the level Marva expected. She asked to redo papers that were not neat enough. When the class was asked to memorize a poem, Erika memorized three. She became addicted to books. One day, after the change had begun to take hold, Marva was asking each child what they had learned on that particular day. "I like Socrates," said Erika. "The only thing I know is how much I don't know. I'm learning something every day." By the end of the school year, Erika was testing at a fourth-grade reading level.

Social skills developed slowly, once the academic skills had begun to formulate. For the other children, Erika's new fanatic enthusiasm to learn was almost as hard to take as her original behavior. Her dramatic social breakthrough came when she accepted the responsibility to tutor new students. Four years after she arrived at Westside Preparatory School as a defeated, broken, asocial, and negative child, Erika McCoy wrote:

> *"If Frederick Douglass can, so can I. If Frederick Douglass could learn when learning seemed impossible for a black man, so can I. If Frederick Douglass can free our people from the bondage of slavery, surely I can free my people from the bondage of ignorance. If Frederick Douglass could conquer the impossible, surely I can conquer ignorance. If Frederick Douglass could deliver speeches to thousands of people, surely I can deliver a speech to the few. If Frederick Douglass could scale the high wall of success, surely I can too."* [28]

The Marva Collins story demonstrates the transforming power of self-respect and its necessary corollary, respect for others. Marva's respect for Erika, evidenced by her desire to help her, drove the child to make a momentous growth decision. When Erika reached for her pencil and began to write her answers, she completed that decision with action. (No decision is complete until it is acted out.) At that pivotal moment, Erika had successfully connected with her inner MetaValues core. That tenuous connection grew stronger as Erika continued to concentrate on Excellence, and later learned Caring and respect for others as she began to tutor other children. Integrity emerged naturally and exponential growth occurred.

Choice and an Impregnable Self-Respect

Consistent growth choices spring from an impregnable self-respect. We can now see that the turning point for Erika came when she was forced to make a growth choice. This single event was enough to break the chain of failures that, otherwise, Erika seemed doomed to continue. Likewise, it was a forced growth choice that changed the life of A. J. Cronin. Most of the remarkable life-changing stories in this book may seem to be the result of an apparent fortuitous intervention, a kind of grace or gift. Sometimes this intervention comes, seemingly out of the blue, as an unexpected insight. At other times, it takes the form of an outside, benevolent personality. Regardless of the form, however, the result is a conscious growth choice followed by an exponential leap in unconscious character growth. This is a microcosm of the self-actualizing process.

One cannot effectively acquire character through the technique of consciously building it. Long lists of desirable character-building qualities are virtually useless by themselves. How, then, does one initiate and maintain the process of self-actualization? By making growth choices that resonate with the MetaValues template of Integrity, Caring, and Excellence—all three action MetaValues balanced in harmonious integration. Upon this simple principle turns the destiny of each human being.

For example, if you are bereft of Integrity in any relationship in your life, attempting to sustain yourself at new levels of performance are doomed to failure. The so-called "shadow of a hair's turning," when contrived to mislead or deceive, is a betrayal of Integrity. It is necessary to correct any existing deception before attempting the processes in this book. The more secrets you have, the more difficult it is to activate the power of MetaValues. A MetaValue growth choice is one that is transparent and strives to move towards the greatest good for all concerned. It is a choice that shuns the easier, softer way, and embraces challenge.

This is not as difficult as it may seem. MetaValues are really a light burden. Using the MetaValues template is challenging, but it makes everything else easier. No longer is an endless process of self-examination and evaluation required. In relative terms, an oak tree seedling is as perfect as a mature and majestic oak specimen. It only lacks what time must supply: maturity and dimension. Likewise, at any stage of actualization we can achieve a dynamic balance of MetaValues. Such a living, upgrasping technique requires constant adjustments and fresh choices as we progress. And we must sacrifice our secrets, and our self-indulgent habits of avoidance, and perhaps our tendency to degrade those we dislike. But the sense of power and freedom that ensues when we jettison these burdens is well worth the cost of giving them up.

The Precious Commodity That Costs Nothing

Does it not seem strange that respect, a force so simple, so powerful and easy to give, is rare and difficult to attain? Respect costs us nothing—any of us can draw upon its power—and yet human attitudes have made respect a rare and unusual commodity. Those times are few in our lives when we have experienced authentic respect—not based upon our status or what we have—but rather on our character and what we can do. Even as you read these words, there are people who are literally dying from lack of respect. The wealthy, the beautiful, the celebrated personalities—all these thirst for an authentic respect, even as we do. Perhaps even more so, because much of the respect the elite experience is an obsequious effort contrived to exploit their power and wealth.

Why is authentic respect so rare? The mystery of the scarcity of respect is shrouded in the great deception that most of us are programmed to live by: if we win enough popularity, publicity, and admiration we will be happy. Most of humanity struggle to gain social status and approval and these are indeed rare and difficult to acquire. In one stratum of society, this deception deludes us into thinking that if we can be smart enough, attractive enough, rich enough, and charismatic enough, we can command genuine respect and admiration. In another stratum, we may be deluded into thinking that if we are strong enough, ruthless enough, and dangerous enough, we will gain attention of another kind—then we will be feared if not respected. In yet another, we may strive for status by complying with demands of others, in being a "good" person. All such strategies are based upon the false premise that there is only so much respect to go around.

"Some estimates indicate that about 90% of the population live in the stew of conformity ... [Most of our lives are] filled with struggle, fear, humiliation, envy, and the endless hungry craving for personal recognition that never leaves us. Even when we are feeding it! ... Exactly those who most of all need to give up this infantile striving for outside recognition they call love are those who find it most impossible to imagine enjoyment in anything apart from being the center of attention." [29]

WILLARD AND MARGUERITE BEECHER
Beyond Success and Failure

The truth is that social approval and recognition are not only difficult to acquire, they are also fleeting and unsatisfying. We need but examine the unhappy, shallow lives of the great majority of those who have achieved the fame and admiration that they coveted. Authentic self-respect is a given; you need not strive for it. You are also naturally empowered to give genuine respect to others. The great paradox is that to maintain self-respect, you must give respect away—to the degree that you respect others, you have an equal capacity to respect yourself.

Respect Will Transform Other People

It took me many years to understand the significance of respecting others. I came to understand that impregnable, unconditional self-respect is a prime requirement, but I did not understand that the capacity for self-respect was limited to the degree we are able to respect others. Every time I built up my self-confidence, it would gradually dissolve away. I wondered why. What happened to my self-respect? Years would go by—many years—before I began to understand. It was my own lack of desire to respect others that deprived me of the very thing I hungered for.

Disrespect takes many forms. It can be blatant or operate behind the mask of the polite deceit of societal process. But more often it manifests as cold, self-contained indifference. In business, in the supermarket, on the sidewalks—we observe unseeing people rush by, manifesting various facades: perhaps they fake confidence and power, or simply manifest indifference and independence. But people are not designed to be at their best as closed systems. Contrary to Freud, love breeds more love, and the spending of love creates a greater wealth of love. Mother Teresa demonstrated this principle by serving the "poorest of the poor" with love and respect in the most terrible slums of India. By giving so generously of unconditional respect, Mother Teresa became one of the most universally respected human beings who ever lived, eventually being honored with the Nobel Peace Prize.

For most of us, the love for humanity does not come easily. Learning the process of love may be set into motion by first granting unconditional respect to each human being we encounter—even strangers. I am not unmindful of the dangerous situations in our cities. But I have known of heroic people who live in the inner cities and who are able to wisely and appropriately manifest respect for their brothers and sisters. Consider the profound influence Marva Collins and Mother Teresa have exerted upon their communities. By what means can we open and broaden our own area of influence to encircle and take in isolated strangers?

I discovered the respect/love alchemy one sun-filled day while I stood in the midst of a crowded county fair in Tulsa. I can still see, in my mind's eye, the bustling and motley crowd of people rushing past in the thick, humid heat of that Oklahoma afternoon. At the time, I had been studying psychology and spiritual techniques and working on my own attitudes for many years. Yet, I felt dismayed as I became aware of the negative feelings that were generated in me by the sight of these ordinary human beings who were simply going about their business.

With increasing annoyance, I found fault with the people going by, their clothing, their faces, their shapes, and their indifferent, brief glances at me as they walked by. It was my custom in those younger years to handle people by quickly mentally rejecting or belittling them—before they could reject me. This technique of evaluating and quickly discounting others (if they appeared to have no apparent power or exploitive value to reckon with) is far more common than most of us imagine. It is a kind of psychic shortcut that we use to avoid the need to think about each encounter. On this particular day, I became disappointed at the programmed negative reaction that was taking place within me. I asked myself, *How will I ever be able to love humanity?*

Suddenly, a remarkable idea came to mind. I decided to respect each of these people. This seemed doable. The idea came from somewhere inside, as a kind of benevolent invasion of my mind and I felt compelled to heed it. So, then and there, I willed a change in my attitude. I turned a respectful eye on the people passing by. I targeted people at random and attempted to make eye contact with them. If I was successful, I sent them a smile and a silent mental message: "I respect you." Very quickly, the people passing by began to transform.

The overdressed woman with too much makeup, the loud teenager with a cigarette hanging out of her mouth, the dirty and ferocious-appearing male who was obviously trying to look as dangerous as possible with his T-shirt sleeves pulled up to reveal his tattoos—each of these people seemed to have a common denominator. Each did (what seemed to me to be) strange things to their appearance and expressed aggressive body language in order to gain some form of respect from others. Let's break down the word "respect" for a second. The prefix "re" means "again." The suffix "spec" means "to look at." Therefore, "respect" means: "Look at me again! Do not dismiss and ignore me! Look again!"

With new eyes, I observed the folks going by. I saw them now, not as arrogant, vain, and dangerous adults, but as young children who hungered for respect. As I observed them from this new perspective, an amazing thing happened. The returned looks—those glances that were, a few seconds before, at least mildly hostile—suddenly transformed. I detected an instant flash, a kind of click in most people as I made eye contact with them and sought to see behind the facade to honor the struggling bit of divinity within. When I did this, people seemed to pause an extra nanosecond or so, and they made a connection with me before they passed by. All of this resulted in a kind of modest peak moment. I knew that my change in attitude had caused something important to happen. I did not know exactly what transformed a negative experience into a tiny but important spiritual breakthrough, but I never forgot the precious happening.

The Power of Relationship

The transformation that took place on that afternoon in Oklahoma was achieved through the process of a change in relationship. Not only did my perception of the people going by change, their reaction to me also underwent a discernable change. The beauty and authentic power of the concept of relationship can be unlocked by a single participant. It requires only one person to change the nature of a relationship—any relationship. In this case I altered my own attitude, and I expanded a circle of respect to take in everyone. By doing this, I truly affected others—I might even have had a beneficial influence upon them. Yet, the greatest benefit was to myself. I felt empowered and exhilarated as I stood there and lavished respect upon the hungry crowd. I got an inkling of what a spiritually enlightened person must feel; I was free of my own ego and fear to a degree I had never known before—and I enjoyed an interlude so replete with spiritual riches that I seemed to have an unlimited amount of respect to bestow to others.

Impregnable self-respect is the first requisite toward self-empowerment. It is the gift that unlocks our human will and energizes our lives. Without authentic self-respect, inner decay sets in. But self-respect cannot maintain itself: authentic self-respect is modulated with micrometer-like precision by the degree of respect we hold for other people. When you are confronted with behavior that is inappropriate and ugly, see the behavior for what it usually is: driven by a hunger for respect. Do not excuse or enable inappropriate and immature behavior, but consider it from the larger perspective and this will help you deal with it without being either provoked or intimidated.

It is true that a constant need for the approval of others is immature. If people could grow into adulthood in a loving environment, they would naturally become loving individuals. Yet, few of us do. Most people are struggling to be loved long after they should be learning to give love. This is true, even though our fulfillment and self-empowerment depends upon our ability to become loving. We may ask ourselves the same question that I asked that fateful Oklahoma afternoon: "How will I ever be able to love humanity?" It becomes clear that we can do so when we understand that virtually every unlovely, immature action or statement we encounter comes from a person who is seeking to be loved long after he should be seeking to love.

The respect/love alchemy I learned at the county fair in Tulsa is a process that can be experienced in a supermarket, a shopping mall, or nearly any crowded place. It requires no special training. Imagine yourself a wealthy person, rich in a commodity that all humans crave and rarely get to enjoy. Since your supply of this commodity is unlimited and since it increases as you give it away, you bestow it upon every individual you see. This energizing exercise in respect should be done continuously, as often as you have the opportunity. It will become a valuable habit and way of life.

Love and respect have been taught by all the enlightened religious sages and teachers down through the ages. Yet hundreds of religious persuasions believe their philosophy is the only one that leads to God. There exist many other less exclusive disciplines, paths, or yogas that claim to lead to enlightenment. Nearly all of these religions and disciplines have a common origin: the *peak experience* by a single enlightened individual. This puzzled Dr. Maslow. He wanted to break down the logic-tight barrier between science and religion. He examined religion and all of its facets in an attempt to make values a tool of science rather than something outside of science and exclusive of it. Maslow wrote:

> *"… this kind of study leads us to another very plausible hypothesis: to the extent that all mystical or peak-experiences are the same in their essence and have always been the same, all religions are the same in their essence and always have been the same … The characteristic prophet is a lonely man who has discovered his truth about the world, the cosmos, ethics, God, and his own identity from within, from his own personal experiences, from what he would consider to be a revelation."* [30]

Labels Divide … MetaValues Unite

We usually divide belief systems into groups, such as religious beliefs, scientific beliefs, and philosophical beliefs. Then we divide them further into types of religious creeds, schools of science, and philosophical systems. These divisions go even further, and subdivide into smaller and smaller groups within a religious sect or a scientific or philosophical belief system. Each belief and discipline has its share of saints and geniuses, as well as kooks and fanatics. We label each group so the people are insulated from other groups and confined to their own. I've illustrated this in *Figure One*.

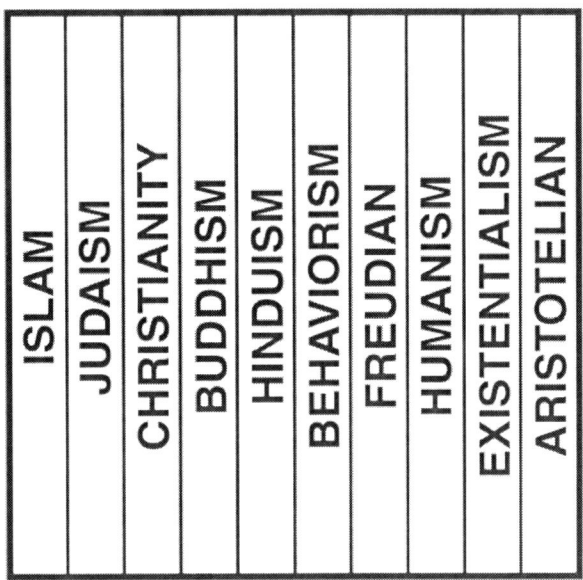

Figure One – Labels Divide

There is another way to look at things. In *Figure Two* you can see that belief systems can also be divided not simply vertically, into sects and subsects of Christianity, Islam, and the various schools of science and philosophy—but also horizontally. These horizontal strata cut through creedal and intellectual divisions and reunify human beings through shared MetaValues. People who are more mature and illuminated by MetaValues (regardless of whether they may have achieved recognition, titles, or authority) are generally tolerant and gracious toward the higher precepts of other beliefs. They are less tolerant toward those—even in their own group—who do not respect the MetaValues of Truth, Beauty, and Goodness. MetaValues even transcend race and gender differences. Labels divide, MetaValues unite.

**Mature individuals
share the same MetaValues
of Truth, Beauty, and Goodness.**

Barriers disappear.

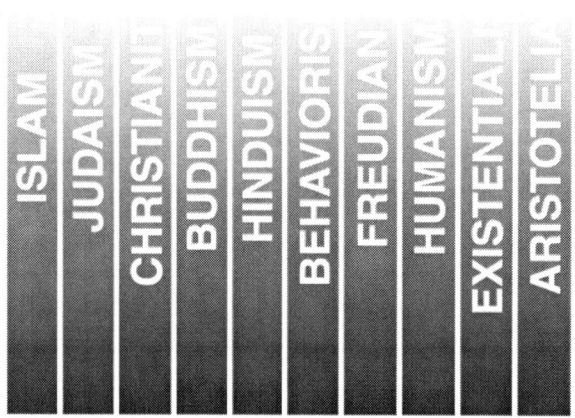

Figure Two – MetaValues Unite

If we "divide" horizontally by MetaValues, many "leaders" will no longer be found in the higher levels. Too many of our leaders do not honor the highest values. In our immature, greedy world, the most aggressive and ruthless people are often the ones who achieve positions of recognition and power. Enlightenment is not necessarily earned by acquiring lofty titles. The genius of the people, the core of shared common values—MetaValues—most often surpasses the teachings of the people's leaders.

Enlightened values are the key to the unity of truth. Enlightened values express the greatest good of all concerned. When scientists are not influenced by MetaValues, they may provide the technology to destroy as efficiently as they provide the technology to bring comfort. When philosophers lose sight of the highest values, they teach systems of despair and cynicism. And when religionists deny the highest knowledge that has been discovered by value-driven scientists and wise philosophers, it may be because they have an emotional investment in outmoded traditions and superstitions. MetaValues are great unifiers, and the enlightened application of MetaValues enriches the religious experience.

I am not proposing that MetaValues will someday unite humanity. Rather, I am suggesting that MetaValues *do* unite mature human beings. It is an observable reality that mature individuals transcend the barriers of labels when they are driven by MetaValues, rather than some blind, adversarial loyalty to a creed or belief. Creedal discussions driven by Integrity, Excellence, and Caring are healing and inclusive. When a claim is made that a particular path or dogma is exclusively correct, conflict is inevitable.

The Self-Actualizer and Religion

The Self-Actualizers Dr. Maslow studied had very personal religious beliefs. He found that they all had transcendent peak experiences. However, they were guarded; they tended not to wish to share them. Although many Actualizers had a formal religion, they had also discovered, developed, and retained their own personal, inner religion. Their inner religion often augmented their formal religion. This concept of a supplementary religion of inner experience contrasted with what Maslow saw as the religious experience of "Sunday only" believers. There is no intervening organization or guru between the Self-Actualizers and their inner religious experience. Maslow saw MetaValues as a path to a different kind of religious experience. This path was *not* in opposition to typical mainstream religious practices, but rather complementary to them. Maslow wrote:

"The forms, rituals, ceremonials, and verbal formulae in which [the profoundly and authentically religious person] was reared remain for him experientially rooted, symbolically meaningful, archetypal, unitive. Such a person may go through the same motions and behaviors as his more numerous co-religionists, but he is never reduced to the merely behavioral, as most of them are." [31]

The disciplines of science, philosophy, and religion ask different questions in their quest for truth. The religionist may perceive MetaValues as originating in the highest power of the universe, and a pathway to a better understanding of God. The philosopher could see MetaValues as factors that will help unify the discoveries of science with enlightened spiritual insights. New levels of efficient living will come about through the unification of idea systems, energy systems, and spiritual systems. Regardless of how MetaValues are defined, ideally they are tools to simplify and integrate humankind's exploding inventory of facts with its highest eternal principles. When thus applied, MetaValues will enhance human life with unprecedented meaning and certainty, and unlock the slumbering genius of the people.

The hope for a better world lies in the personal maturity and growth of each individual. When we achieve personal self-respect and learn to sustain it by lavishing respect and love upon others, we are poised to move to another level of personal development. And then we are confronted by a new challenge: responsibility for the inner life. Your inner-life experience is determined by your attitudes. But most people are hampered by the conviction that they have been victimized by others. We all are likely to harbor resentments that seem totally justified. Many indulge in replaying personal soap operas, bitter episodes, and fantasies of revenge. But just as the law of gravity cannot be successfully defied, so the law of resentments will weaken and defeat any effort we make toward self-empowerment. How, then, can we take charge of the inner life and create it according to our highest desires? We'll discuss that in the next chapter.

TAKING ACTION

Practice unconditional respect. It is an active exercise that you can perform with all of your relationships. Active respect can be practiced on passersby in any reasonably normal situation. This is an excellent *reminding factor*—you are automatically operating on a higher level of consciousness when you practice unconditional, active respect. Begin to look at everyone as though you actually *see* them. By *Caring* about people on a higher level, you are also demonstrating the critical MetaValue of *Goodness*.

We now have two action-items going on. In addition to active respect, you are anticipating success by writing your own headlines and doing an action review at the end of the day. This demonstrates *Excellence*. By the simple acts of actually doing these things, you demonstrate *Integrity*. It is impossible to engage all three MetaValues in an active manner and not operate on a higher level of consciousness. Sustaining these simple tasks requires almost constant focus … you will no longer be living on automatic. You have set the breakthrough into motion.

CHAPTER FOUR
Relinquishing Victimhood

"… man is the master of thought, the molder of character, and the maker and shaper of condition, environment, and destiny. As a being of Power, Intelligence, and Love, and the lord of his own thoughts, man holds the key to every situation, and contains within himself that transforming and regenerative agency by which he may make himself what he wills." [32]

JAMES ALLEN
As A Man Thinketh

Viktor Frankl considered how unjustly life had victimized him and his family. Not long before, Frankl had been a promising and prosperous psychiatrist, the head of the Neurology Department of the Rothschild Hospital in his beautiful native Vienna. Now he had become number 119,104—first in Theresienstadt, then successively in Auschwitz, Kaufering III, and Türkheim. Every possession he owned had been confiscated. Today was his beloved wife's birthday, yet he did not even know whether she was still alive. The "crime" of Frankl and his family had been discovered: they were Jews, and for that, they were imprisoned in a Nazi death camp. [33]

As Viktor Frankl shivered in the frigid Auschwitz rain, the terrifying four A.M. roll call interrupted his confused thoughts like intermittent daggers. He stared at one of his rain-saturated shoes and the fragment of wire that was serving as a shoestring for one of them. Through his aching hunger, he realized he must replace it soon. Already he felt the terrible sores on his feet beginning to bleed. Frankl was disturbed that after all of his hard work, at the age of thirty-seven, his life had been reduced to worrying about pieces of wire and crusts of bread. The realization opened the doors of despair. But he refused to yield.

From someplace in the depths of his soul, a vision began to form. Suddenly, with a clarity that startled him, Frankl saw himself in a bright, warm lecture room. In front of him, an audience listened attentively as they sat in their comfortably upholstered seats. Frankl heard himself giving a lecture on the psychology of death camp life.

Frankl realized that he somehow was transcending the unbearable sufferings of the moment and he was observing them as though they had taken place in the remote past. Viktor Frankl was experiencing a miracle of the human will—that manifestation of the human mind that enables the subjective self to transcend present consciousness and to creatively and objectively propose a better future.

As he stood in formation among the living dead, Frankl realized that he wanted to live. He must live to fulfill his vision; then his hopeless suffering of the present would have meaning. He decided to live so that others would learn of what had happened. Then, perhaps, it would never happen again. But Frankl knew it would not be easy to survive Auschwitz. Only three or four out of a hundred were able to endure the death camps. And most of these survivors were the dreaded Capos—prisoners who cooperated with their captors by becoming ruthless straw bosses, enforcers, and informants. Others subsisted by playing on their professional skills. Although Frankl was trained medically and occasionally served as a physician, he had elected not to try to become a camp doctor. He would live or die as an ordinary prisoner.

"Life Has Nothing to Offer Me Anymore"

Viktor Frankl recalled that before prisoners in the camp died, they behaved according to a clear pattern. Prior to the point when they physically died, they became one of the living dead. They began to indulge themselves and they quit scheming to save a crust of bread for the future. They would smoke all their precious few cigarettes, and they would nearly always make the same declaration of despair: *"Life has nothing to offer me anymore."*

A gust of icy air whipped through the ranks, but Frankl barely noticed. Another fresh insight formed in his mind. He thought about the dying prisoners who lamented that life no longer had any meaning. He wondered, *What does one do when life no longer has any meaning?* Then the answer dawned on him. Frankl realized that the question, "What is the meaning of life?" is not a question that human beings should ask. It is rather a question that they must answer! Life itself asks the compelling question, "What is the meaning of life?" and we answer that question, not in words, but by our attitudes and how we live.

Frankl now grasped that our reason for being is to give meaning to life. If we can establish this meaning, this *why* to live, we will find the means to survive. A human being with a reason to live is empowered to discover the *way* to live. Now Viktor Frankl knew the ultimate key to freedom. It was attitude. The hope-inspiring, creative thoughts that were now running through his mind were possible, in spite of all he had lost, because he had retained a singular power. The Nazis had taken everything—his family, his home, his possessions (including a precious manuscript that represented his life's work). They had taken his profession and indeed were capable at any moment of taking his life, but they could never take from him his right to choose his attitude toward the situation he was in. And because he retained the power of attitude, he could still set goals. Frankl still possessed the ability to creatively reframe the predicament that confronted him to give it meaning. He did this by embellishing his vision, his goal, his impossible dream.

Frankl concluded that he must live—not only to tell the world about the death camps, but also to tell humankind that they have the power of choice. They can choose to shut down and quit, or they can assume responsibility for living lives of meaning and purpose. Anyone can set into motion a creative and inspiring answer to the question "What is the meaning of my life?"

Frankl intuitively knew that this monumental insight would be lost if he failed to act upon it. So he set about to reconstruct his life's work—he coveted tiny scraps of paper, and during his three years of imprisonment he recalled and wrote down the key words and phrases of his destroyed manuscript. He hid these in cracks in the wall of the hut where he lived. He began to act out, to live, the basic principles of his life's work. In addition to reconstructing his original manuscript, Frankl formed clear and detailed images of the lectures he would one day deliver and he rehearsed them repeatedly in his mind. He also realized that if he allowed himself to give way to malice and resentment, he would deplete his energies and weaken his chances to survive. So he refused to succumb to hate and victimhood. While he poured his heart into achieving his vision, he also focused upon every positive aspect of camp life he could.

The Unconquerable Human Spirit

The Nazi death camps were designed to distort and reconfigure human behavior. The culture of the camps savagely tore away the masks of socialized personality; prisoners and guards alike were psychologically naked before one another. The most uplifting, inspiring, and saintly qualities in humans were revealed—along with the most evil, depraved, and disgusting. Frankl recalled Freud's cynical comment that such conditions blur the differences in humans and they all act as savages. Frankl believed that such ideas may be easy to espouse to a patient lying upon a plush couch in a comfortable, warm room in Vienna. But amid the lice and vermin and pestilence of Auschwitz, he had learned the truth: the human spirit often succumbs to such deprivation, but this inner force also (though admittedly less often) can rise above unthinkable circumstances. In the same manner as Abraham Maslow, Frankl observed that Freudian ideas could not explain these exceptional manifestations of the invincible human spirit.

Frankl saw and honored the exceptions in the camp that proved the noble spirit of humanity. Frankl thus learned to love and respect all of those trapped in this grotesque drama, including the guards and Capos who might, upon occasion, show shreds of sanity and decency. He continually sought the opportunity to do small acts of kindness to help and encourage other prisoners. He urged them to continue the struggle. Frankl sought to experience and honor important values through his daily living. Viktor Frankl would one day describe the process of sharing the highest human values of Truth, Beauty, Goodness, and Love in these words:

> *"... by experiencing something—such as goodness, truth, and beauty—by experiencing nature and culture or, last but not least, by experiencing another human being in his uniqueness—by loving him ... by love [we are] enabled to see the essential traits and features in the beloved person; and even more, to see that which is potential in him; which is not yet actualized but which ought to be actualized ... By making him aware of what he can be and of what he should become, [we help make] these potentialities come true."* [34]

Frankl understood the grim day-to-day realities of the situation he was coping with. Regardless of what he did, he knew that he would need a huge measure of luck if he were to survive. Frankl did not minimize the horror of the camp by avoiding problems or harboring illusions. The situation was life and death; he had to face it without flinching. Yet he believed his best chance of survival was to remind himself continually of the one factor he could control: *his attitude.*

Viktor Frankl survived and carried through on his vision of telling the world about the Holocaust. He redeveloped his original work around the theme of humankind's intrinsic Will-to-Meaning—a system he termed *Logotherapy.* His seventeen books, and his countless articles and lectures have been translated into several languages. He made dozens of visits to the United States, spoke on college campuses, and was quite active until his death in 1997.

To the reader who may imagine that his or her situation is too mundane and ordinary to have meaning, in his most famous book, *Man's Search for Meaning*, Frankl leaves this admonition:

> *"Do not think that these considerations are unworldly and too far removed from real life. It is true that ... of the prisoners only a few kept their full inner liberty and obtained those values which their suffering afforded, but even one such example is sufficient proof that man's inner strength may raise him above his outward fate. Such men are not only in concentration camps."* [35]

It is true that "only a few" keep their "inner liberty." The message to take home is that each of us can be one of those few. We can elevate our consciousness regardless of our outer circumstances. Frankl did this. He proved that it is possible to take everything from an individual except one thing: *his right to choose his attitude toward any given situation.* Thus, the will is the determining factor for the inner life experience and each of us is responsible for the nature of our wills. Frankl shunned victimhood and exerted his will to convert a hopeless situation into something of supreme meaning. A single drop of self-pity can sicken the mind for hours. When self-pity becomes a habit, it can lead to deep trauma and even self-destruction. For example, consider the little-known experience of Buckminster Fuller. Few know that the renowned inventor of the geodesic dome nearly committed suicide as a young man.

The Transformation of Buckminster Fuller

"Bucky" Fuller, born in 1895, gained fame as an architect, engineer, futurist, cartographer, writer, and poet. During the '20s, he coined the term Spaceship Earth, and was the first to write of the problems of a closed-system planet. In 1969, he was nominated for the Nobel Peace Prize. Yet, most people have forgotten what is probably his most astounding achievement. This lost achievement is the MetaValues insight he had as a young man that saved him from suicide and propelled him on a fast track to world fame and accomplishment.[36]

In 1927, Fuller was an abject failure, penniless and without hope. He and his wife were living in Chicago in a one-room apartment on Belmont Avenue. For five years, the Fullers had been grieving the tragic loss of their first child. The child had suffered through bouts with infantile paralysis, flu, spinal meningitis, and pneumonia. After her long ordeal and struggle, on her fourth birthday, she breathed her final breath. It was a crushing, devastating loss. Fuller buried himself in a flurry of activity. He assisted his architect father-in-law in creating a company based upon a new building material. Fuller organized four factories around the country to produce the new product. He worked at a manic pace, but the pain of his lost child would not go away. The minute Fuller got through work for the day, he went off to drink all night. His new enterprise tanked. He felt disgraced; several investors had lost money on the project. Just as he was hitting bottom, a new daughter was born to the Fullers, Allegra. *Am I an utter failure?* Fuller asked himself. *If so, I had better get myself out of the way, so at least my wife and baby can be taken care of by my family.*

On this fateful night, Fuller made his way to Lincoln Park, right on the shores of Lake Michigan. He knew the park well. At night, he would run through the park and spend hours lamenting his fate. Tonight he had a special plan in mind. He would hurl himself into the water and end his life. Standing at the shoreline, something made him hesitate. Now, in what he thought would be the last few moments of his life, he began to ask questions from the depths of his soul. He suddenly realized that all his life he had taken advice from others; he had never trusted his own mind. He wondered what importance a small, impoverished man with a remaining life expectancy of only ten more years could have anyway. (Fuller was thirty-two and the life expectancy of those born in 1895 was only forty-two.) The big corporations and powerful governments seemed unable to solve the planet's problems. So, what significance could he possibly have?

From somewhere within, answers began to come to Fuller. *The individual can take initiatives without anyone's permission,* he thought. Then he said something astonishing to himself:

> *"You do not have the right to eliminate yourself, you do not belong to you. You belong to the universe. The significance of you will forever remain obscure to you, but you may assume that you are fulfilling your significance if you apply yourself to converting all your experience to the highest advantage of others."*

These transforming words startled Fuller. The strangely worded sentence could have but one meaning. He was to *convert* his entire life experience to one of service. He vowed from that moment to live—but to live in an entirely new way. Never again would he live only for himself. He would use his unfinished life to serve humankind. He also vowed to do his own thinking instead of trying to accommodate everyone else's opinions, credos, and theories. He determined to use all of his powers toward solving the problems that affect everyone aboard planet Earth. He concluded that if he forgot himself and worked only for all humanity, he would be doing what nature wanted him to do and that nature would support him in this.

Buckminster Fuller left the park and returned home a transformed man. Fuller did not want to waste a second. He began sleeping just one half hour every six hours. He decided to forget about earning a living and to commit himself to the creation of things to help the ecology of planet Earth. His was the path of service, the conversion of all experience toward the benefit of others. In one of the rare times he ever addressed a religious issue, Fuller the scientist decided to do his own thinking about whether a higher power existed or not. He asked himself:

> *"Do you have any experiential evidence that forces you to assume a greater intellect operating in the universe? My answer was swift and positive. Experience demonstrated an orderliness of interactive, exceptionless principles. I was overwhelmed by this, and more convinced that my purpose was to abet the inclusion of human beings in the design of the universe. I'm absolutely convinced that everything that has happened to me since that time has been through my commitment to this greater integrity. Many times I've chickened, and everything inevitably goes wrong. But then, when I return to my commitment, my life suddenly works again. There's something of the miraculous in that."*

The "interactive, exceptionless principles" that Fuller connected to were MetaValues. Over the next fifty-four years (well beyond his life expectancy), Buckminster Fuller went on to blaze a career of unparalleled achievements. He would author twenty-eight books and receive forty-seven honorary doctorates in the arts, science, engineering, and the humanities. Fuller would be awarded dozens of major architectural and design awards including the Gold Medal of the American Institute of Architects and the Gold Medal of the Royal Institute of British Architects. He would acquire twenty-eight U.S. patents for his inventions. Bucky kept his vow and committed his entire productivity to the whole planet Earth and its resources, undertaking to protect and advance all life forms. He often stated that he found greater effectiveness in his work when devoting it entirely to the service of others.

There could be no question of Fuller's integrity and excellence. But perhaps the greatness of the man is illustrated best by his goodness. Here is one of my favorite stories about Buckminster Fuller, as related by his daughter, Allegra Fuller Snyder:

> *"My father was a warm, concerned, and sharing father. As focused as he was on his own work, he nevertheless included me in his experiences and experiencing. I remember with great clarity when I was about four years old. I was sick in bed and he was taking care of me. He sat down on the bed beside me, with his pencil in hand, and told me, through wonderful free-hand drawings, a Goldilocks story. I was Goldilocks and with his pencil he transported me, not to the Bear's house, but to the universe, to help me understand something of Einstein's Theory of Relativity. What he was telling me was neither remote nor abstract. I was in a newly perceived universe. I was experiencing my father's*

thoughts and he was experiencing his own thinking as he communicated with me. It was exciting. We were sharing something together and I felt very warm and close to him in that experience." [37]

Buckminster Fuller accomplished all of these things after first making an irrevocable decision to relinquish victimhood and live a life of service. By abandoning concern about self and focusing upon serving others, he set the self-actualization process into motion. The service motive is the fastest and most reliable path to enlightenment and actualization. The formula is simple, but few have dared to apply it wholeheartedly to their own careers.

The Martyrdom Paradox

Why does most of humanity find claiming the status of victim so irresistible? What is the payoff? If "martyr-medals" were awarded to all the people who believed themselves to be victims in life, nearly everyone would get one. Not only weaklings and losers, many of our "toughest" leaders—when defeated or losing confidence, or unhappy with a situation, or when failing to live up to their potentials— claim to be the victim of others. Rarely do we humans concede that we own the lion's share of the blame for our failures; seldom do we admit to being at fault. You need go no further than your own experience to validate the chronic search for excuses and scapegoats. Listen to the daily conversations around you. Monitor your own excuses. Hear the complaints at lunch counters, in the subways, and in the break rooms. The opiate of the modern masses is this pseudo martyrdom, the denial or avoidance of responsibility for the inner life. Why? Consider the distinct advantages of being a victim:

- Being a victim assures us of being innocent; we are not responsible for the way our lives are turning out.
- As victims, we have the delicious right to complain, gripe, and rail at circumstances and people.
- As victims, we are granted the rights of boundless self-pity.
- Accepting victimhood solves the question of right or wrong: we are innocent victims, and thus we are right. The people and things that thwarted us are, of course, wrong.

However, despite these advantages, the price for embracing martyrdom is high. By shifting the responsibility for our lives to others, we also, by default, hand over authority. This is a price the Self-Actualizer will not—cannot—accept. For, not withstanding the advantages of victimhood, no other attitude is more certain to insure a life of mediocrity. Those who shroud themselves in the mantle of victimhood live joyless, soap-opera lives because they've deprived themselves of the freedom to seize the moment. Resentment, anger, regret, fear, guilt—all of these things pull them out of the present and into the regretful past or the threatening future. What is needed is freedom from the tyranny of victimhood and self-pity. What is needed is the assumption of self-mastery and responsibility. Sooner or later, in every worthy life, there must come that supreme moment—the moment of assumption of responsibility:

> *I am a free human being. I am not a victim. I live in the environment I do, I am where I am in life, I associate with the people I do, have the attitudes I have, because of circumstances I have created or permitted to exist. I am capable of achieving whatever I can intelligently determine to achieve, and I am responsible for my life.*

No one can rescue me, but mighty forces will come to my aid when I begin to make growth decisions and complete them through positive actions.

Your Most Important Power

Viktor Frankl discovered the creative power within that can give life meaning and purpose. It is perhaps the most important power you possess. You can lose it, or waste it, but no one can take this power away from you. Animals cannot give life meaning; they cannot envision a better way to live. But we can exert our will to give our life intention and purpose, we can turn on the lights and tap into the same limitless energy that drives the universe. This philosophy admonishes us to refuse to accept anything less than an inner life of supreme significance.

All of us are naturally endowed with the power to become a benevolent creative force in the universe. The universe instantly rushes to the aid of those who decide to actualize that power. The universe is not an impersonal, materialistic machine destined to crush the human spirit. It is more like the creative mind of the individual who seeks its secrets and its meaning. Because the universe needs help as it strives to evolve toward perfection, it responds to the faintest flicker of willingness to participate and assist in its quest. This is why the passionate vision of those who strive to serve others apparently overcomes all obstacles and achieves virtual miracles.

A. J. Cronin's story of his first novel demonstrated the power of the Will-to-Fail, the Jonah Complex. It showed how we all have the vestiges of self-doubt, a certain lack of self-respect. A sublime sense of self-respect will sustain us through each challenge, including the final moment of chaos that inevitably comes just before we break through our personal limitations and succeed. However, the unavoidable rule of self-respect decrees that we cannot respect ourselves to a greater degree than we respect others. Marva Collins actually transformed the lives of the children she taught by lavishing respect and love upon them. We, too, have the power to transform other lives and, by doing so, transform ourselves.

For those who are certain that their situation is hopeless and void of options, we have the awesome example of Viktor Frankl. He demonstrated the remarkable power of the human will to propose a vision of a better way, the way that ought to be. In the face of devastating depravation, Frankl accepted the reality of his situation, and proved that the will to live springs forth from the discovery of a why to live. And Frankl shows us that the question, *What is the meaning of life?* is a question we are to answer, not ask.

Finally, Buckminster Fuller found himself by losing himself in service to humankind. His simple resolution to convert all of his experience to the highest advantage of others completely revolutionized his life.

All of the above episodes illustrate the power of the human will to overcome the blocks that prevent self-actualization. What man and woman have done, man and woman can do. We can all live lives of responsibility and respect. We can all assume the task of clearing out the baggage that prevents an inner life of freedom and limitless possibility. We can all develop a will to execute unconditional respect upon all those we encounter. And we can all find ourselves by losing ourselves in service to humankind. Where there is a why to live, there we will find the way to live.

Men and Women of La Mancha

I have long been enthralled by the story of Don Quixote. Possibly because the idea of roaming the sunlit plains of Spain in search of the "Impossible Dream" appealed to me, especially as a youngster.

In the musical interpretation, *Man of la Mancha*, Don Quixote leaves his estate and embarrasses his family as he wanders the land in rusty armor and sees only good around him. The family conspires to bring him home. They send a materialistic doctor and a priest, who finally track him down and confront him. After some unfruitful discussion, the doctor exclaims, *"Don Quixote! You must come to terms with life as it is!"* The Don's reply is memorable:

> *"I have lived nearly fifty years, and I have seen life as it is. Pain, misery, hunger, cruelty beyond belief. I have heard the singing from taverns and the moans from bundles of filth on the streets. I have been a soldier and seen my comrades fall in battle, or die more slowly under the lash in Africa. I have held them in my arms at the final moment. These were men who saw life as it is, yet they died despairing... their eyes filled with confusion, whimpering the question: 'Why?' I do not think they asked why they were dying, but why they had lived. When life itself seems lunatic, who knows where madness lies? ... To surrender dreams—this may be madness. To seek treasure where there is only trash. Too much sanity may be madness. And maddest of all, to see life as it is and not as it ought to be!"* [38]

The Great Price of Self-Actualization

The world needs more men and women of La Mancha. Even today, far too many die in spirit and mind long before their bodies die. The world needs individuals who dare, as Viktor Frankl dared, to see things as they ought to be—even when confronted by injustice and suffering. In the face of a society that seems owned and driven by forces of greed, power, and indifference, it takes a supreme courage to honor the highest human values, the MetaValues of Truth, Beauty, Goodness, and Love. And indeed, the price is high for those who dare to leave the ranks of the living dead and fight for some ideal or mission of service that is more important than themselves. But the rewards of rising above mediocrity are wonderful and rich beyond all description. So important are these rewards that we will revisit the theme of MetaValues service several times as we push forward into the boundless frontiers of self-actualization.

The greatest story of all has not yet been told. This is the yet-to-be-written story of your life. No matter what you have been through, or what you have lost, it is what you have left that matters. The remaining pages of your story are as white as snow.

Still, some will insist, *My own case is unique. I am damaged goods. My entire psyche has been violated and distorted. Am I to believe that a connection with MetaValues can heal anything? I have been to therapist after therapist with no relief, or temporary improvements at best. How am I to believe this promise?* If you are one of these people, perhaps you, like Buckminster Fuller, are standing at the edge of hopelessness.

You too can set up circumstances that provide the necessary opening for MetaValues to work. I can also state with utter conviction that—however you may transcend your personal chasm of doubt—there is peace beyond understanding on the other side. Virtually all of us have been victims. We have legitimate issues that are difficult to resolve. Over the years, I have developed a process that has helped many people free themselves of deeply seated resentments. This process is a hybrid technique, combining things I learned in group therapy with the concepts of Maslow, Frankl, and other great minds. I will offer it to you in the next chapter.

TAKING ACTION

Remember, you can take action without anyone's permission. Begin striving to convert all of your experience to the highest advantage of others. This remarkable philosophy is a powerful technique of taking active respect to another level. Couple this with anticipation of success (writing your own headlines). If you do these things with uncompromising integrity, the body will be energized and the inner life will take care of itself.

CHAPTER FIVE
The Road Not Traveled

"In a few hundred years, when the history of our time will be written from a long-term perspective, it is likely that the most important event historians will see is not technology, not the Internet, not e-commerce. It is an unprecedented change in the human condition. For the first time—literally—substantial and rapidly growing numbers of people have choices. For the first time, they will have to manage themselves. And society is totally unprepared for it." [39]

PETER F. DRUCKER
Leader to Leader

Many years ago, a sage named Rick Strauss disclosed a legend about a group of travelers who sought to climb a mighty mountain. They were making good progress in their climb and soon came in sight of the summit of the mountain. About the same time, they noted that a powerful storm was raging just above them, and they would have to pass through it to reach their goal.

Fortunately, the travelers observed that there was a cabin close by. They entered, and were delighted to find that it was warm, comfortable, and well stocked with food and fresh water. They decided it would be wise to delay their trip until the storm abated.

The tourists enjoyed the security and serenity of the cabin, and several days went by. But not all of them were completely at ease. Some sensed that they should be doing something other than enjoying the comfort of their sanctuary. Occasionally, a few of the travelers went outside and noted the shining pinnacle of the mountain, bright in the sunlight above the storm. But, although the great goal beckoned them, the storm raged on. After weeks had passed, an old native to the area happened by. He asked them why they were staying in the cabin. The travelers explained that they were waiting for the storm near the summit of the mountain to end, so they could continue their journey. The native smiled. He told the pilgrims that there was always a storm near the summit of the mountain.

Even though all of us are being called, the truth is that ninety-nine percent or so of humanity are fearfully huddled together in a conspiracy of mediocrity. How did so many of us get into this predicament? Perhaps because, for centuries, the masses of humankind have been sold short. We have been programmed to believe that we are very restricted in our choices. Now, more and more of us perceive an authentic degree of freedom to shape our destinies. And Drucker is right; we were not educated nor prepared for this moment of truth.

Knowing that the shackles have been removed and the prison door has been unlocked, the masses still languish, afraid to push that door open and leave their comfort zones. Why? Because the path we are being called to is not only "the road less traveled"—it is the road that has never been traveled at all. We are called to blaze an utterly new path, to break new snow. On this path, we will learn that the feelings of numbing tentativeness and impending doom are not natural states. They exist only in the dead center of indecision.

Growth decisions, however modest at first, move us instantly toward a life of joy, rich new relationships, and endless possibilities.

The fortunate few—the Frankls, Fullers, and Marva Collinses who have dared to sally forth into the storms of sublime uncertainty, depending solely upon their own inner power-connection—have sometimes reported their stories back to us. We learn that these people are not very different from us. Often, they disclose in their stories that they did not willingly take up the challenge; more commonly it was apparent chance circumstances that pushed them out the door. We are surprised to learn that life isn't really any easier for those living on the edge than it is for us. What is different about their lives is the inner spirit that drives, inspires, and energizes them. This spirit drives those who live lives of uncompromising Integrity; who produce with continually improving Excellence; and who relate to others with tireless, passionate Caring and respect. And they do all of this with a gracious, exquisite balance of confidence and love.

In this new way of living, there is no room for fear or indifference. Self-Actualizers face life, ready for anything. Unlike most of us, they seem to relish uncertainty, apparent defeat generates enthusiasm, and when they are confronted with insurmountable problems, they are not intimidated; they are energized. Remarkable paradoxes seem to operate in this unfolding realm of freedom. Safety and stability lie in movement, in embracing adventures of extravagant risk. Strength and greatness are demonstrated by forbearance and goodness.

We are advised by those pilgrims who have blazed their own paths: Do not harbor safe goals. Rather, dream outrageous dreams. Announce plans that will awaken the sleeping minds of strangers and that startle those who know you. In liaison with MetaValues, any dream or vision that the world has need of—absolutely anything that ought to be—is possible.

Blazing the Path Not Traveled

What are the odds that you will be one of those who are plucked out of the humdrum masses and thrust into a new way of life? If you are not, can you muster the strength to go forth on your own? Can you sustain your motivation and courage when you breach the unknown? I am absolutely convinced all of us can.

Although you have been underestimated, you need never spend another moment buying into that evaluation. What you sense deep in your soul is real. And if you will follow me through the processes in these pages, the day will come when those powers that are faintly stirring deep within you grow to become more real and important than all the stuff you have been told. The forces you sense within are abiding and eternal. And they will never let you down.

In reality, there is really nothing out there blocking any of us. As mentioned before, there are rather three broad areas of our nondevelopment—immaturity—that cripple us. And these are the failure to master the respect paradox, the failure to assume responsibility for the inner life, and the failure to make growth choices. All three are failures of the human will. All are subject to our conscious control.

Before we can operate at full throttle, we must meet our normal biological needs for nutrition, sleep, and exercise. Then we must feel safe and have a sense of belonging. We must feel respected and appreciated. We must also have reached a point of spiritual advantage in which we no longer feel compelled to take something from the world in an attempt to feel fulfilled. We are comfortable in our own skin, and enjoy an abundant sense of love flowing from the universe.

A new need arises now to share the abundance within with the world. The need to be loved has been supplanted by a passion to love and serve. From the success of Marva Collins's students, we see evidence that if people could grow into adulthood in a loving environment, they would naturally become caring and productive individuals. Virtually every distasteful thing people do is the result of struggling to obtain respect long after they should be learning to give it. This lack of love and respect generates an insatiable need in immature adults for attention and appreciation.

So it is that most of us are self-absorbed in our search for recognition. Victor Frankl once pointed out that the human eye sees perfectly when it is healthy, unaware of itself. But if the eye is diseased, it sees itself, and this clouds its view of what is out there in the world. Likewise, a human ego that is constantly aware of itself— or trying to fix itself or other people––exists in a tedious, immature, less-than-healthy state. Such a person often exerts superhuman efforts to bend the realities of the universe to meet his desires. Yet, he could achieve far more with a fraction of the effort by learning to conform with the cosmic flow. The great mystery of self-actualization is that it takes place unconsciously, while we are absorbed in doing something else. By acquiring respect for others, we escape the needy confines of self-absorption. By abandoning fanatic dedication to self, we find ourselves—and set the self-actualizing process into motion.

The Untapped Creative Power of the Inner Life

It is a profound truth that the inner life of men and women is truly creative. We are very rarely told of this truth, nor are we trained to utilize it. Most of us grow up assuming that we have no control over our thoughts. As a result, we squander the creative possibilities of the mind. Most minds are preoccupied by prejudice, hate, fears, resentments, revenge, and bigotries. Rarely do we learn to exercise dominion over mind.

When I was a young man, I had an experience that gave me my first inkling of what it feels like to have power over thought and a deep sense of self. When I made this discovery, I was certain I had found the secret of the universe. I had yet to learn that having knowledge of something is not the same as knowing it or owning it. We really do not own something until we incorporate it into our experience and share it with others. Yet, even though I would find it necessary to retrace my steps time and again and relearn the value of self-mastery, the original experience was a critical beginning. It was my introduction to the power of mind control and self-induced inner peace.

As an eighteen-year-old, I lived in a dysfunctional home. I was angry, poor, and had little hope. In this shadowy world, there were many temptations and diversions, but few positive possibilities. Or so it seemed. Too bored and indifferent to study, I barely managed to graduate from high school. Soon, I was working as a laborer in a local lumberyard. On the surface, I appeared defiant and confident, but inside I was in constant fear, turmoil, and despair. It was as though I was not really fully awake and was watching the world through a long tunnel. Then, I happened into a barbershop and met a man known in the neighborhood as "Don the Barber." From there, everything began to change.

A haircut was a rare occasion for me in those days. I had passed the tiny barbershop many times, but had never entered it before. Don was middle-aged and walked with a severe limp. His intensity and friendliness immediately struck me as unusual. We were alone in the shop, and as he cut my hair, he talked about mind power, human will, and other subjects that seemed peculiar to me. I could not imagine why he wanted to discuss such offbeat ideas with me. I answered most of his overtures and questions with a grunt or a few mumbled words.

When I paid this unusual man, he suddenly handed me a small book with a worn blue cover. I turned the old tome over in my hands and noted the title: *Raja Yoga … or Mental Development*, by Yogi Ramacharaka. "Why don't you read this book, and tell me what you think?" he suggested. In those days, such books were unusual in our culture. I was deeply suspicious. A yogi, to me, was a skinny guy with a turban who could lie upon a bed of nails.

"You don't believe all this stuff, do you?" I asked.

He smiled. "Well, just read it. Think of it as a cafeteria of ideas. If one appeals to you, take it. Otherwise, pass it by."

I tucked the book under my arm and promised to return it. When I got home, I decided to look the book over. I began to read by the afternoon light of my window. I read words unlike anything I had ever read before: *"Before man attempts to solve the secrets of the Universe without, he should master the Universe within—the Kingdom of the Self."* [40]

For a young man who had concluded he was fighting a losing battle with a hostile universe, the concept of a refuge within—a Kingdom of Self—was irresistible. The idea that there is another, better self within, with access to powerful resources unavailable to my present state of consciousness, was thrilling. It seemed to me that I had been playing a life role far below my capacities, one I did not relish. Down deep, I wanted to be something else. Raja Yoga declared that my "real" self was hidden by the fake outer persona, a facade that I presented to the world so that I could cope and get along. I was even more astounded by the assertion that it was possible for any normal person to control the mind and achieve inner peace. The idea that I could control thought was completely unique to me. The greatest of all demoralizers is the state of being in which we are helpless victims of our thoughts.

Regarding the many grievances that tortured my mind, I read:

> *"Yet this is an absurd position—for man, the heir of all the ages: hag-ridden by the flimsy creatures of his own brain … It should be as easy to expel an obnoxious thought from your mind as it is to shake a stone out of your shoe; and till a man can do that it is just nonsense to talk about his ascendancy over Nature, and all the rest of it. He is a mere slave, and prey to the bat-winged phantoms that flit through the corridors of his own brain. Yet the weary and careworn faces that we meet by the thousands, even among the affluent classes of civilization, testify only too clearly how seldom this mastery is obtained. How rare indeed to meet a MAN!"*
> 41

I read and read. I was unaware of time or space. When the light from the window was so dim I could not read anymore, I looked up and observed the dark disorder I lived in. *There is a better way to live*, I thought. Of course, I knew that if I had money I could live on a higher material level. But the stunning new idea was: *There is a better way to live now*. I could create my own world within! It could be my own gallery of peace, freedom, and joy. I reasoned that if my mind could generate and sustain thoughts as clear and pure as a mountain stream, no one could hurt me anymore. No matter what others did, they could not destroy, or even affect, my inner kingdom—unless I let them. It all seemed so simple.

The pivotal, enduring insight I gleaned that day was this assurance that I had choices. I gained the knowledge that no matter what circumstances surrounded me, I could master my inner life. At the time, I had no idea how difficult such inner mastery would turn out to be. It would take the better part of a lifetime and what seemed to be endless grief before I could consistently win the battle within. Even so, in times of despair, the original revelation that we can control our thoughts gave me hope. That day, I also accepted responsibility for the secret place, my inner life. The strange book that Don the Barber lent me made me conscious of self, of being, in a way I had never imagined before.

Later, I would learn that Third Force psychology is based upon the principle that we are responsible for what we think. We cannot blame anyone else for our emotions, moods, and negative thoughts. Psychologists have also generally agreed that there is a place of peace within the human psyche that seems relatively insulated from outer circumstances. Viktor Frankl believed that this inner place, what he called the irreducible essence, is a core reality that provides the basis for human will and a continuity of consciousness. One way we experience this reality is through the belief we all share that we are the same inner person who experienced our childhood and all the incidents of our past. (In fact, most of us intuit the reality of self—and the reality of relationships with other people—as realities that transcend all other realities.)

Two renowned psychologists of Maslow's era, Willard and Marguerite Beecher, expressed this idea of a shared inner reality of being in this way:

> *"We somehow are not surprised when we are told for the first time that at the eye of the hurricane is total calm ... We know that somewhere inside of us we are at peace. Our only problem is to discover what prevents us from getting to this center-of-our-being and holding on to it. The question in our mind is why we cannot live at this core easily, as we know it must be possible for a man to do."* [42]

We do not have to create this place of peace. It is there for us. If we can learn to "live at this core," as the Beechers suggest, we will find ourselves safely in a place of considerable spiritual advantage. From this core of peace, there are virtually no inhibitions restricting the creative function of the inner life. When we allow our consciousness to lose hold of this objective advantage, we are soon caught up in the tumultuous stream of our reactive, uncontrolled thoughts and emotions. Such inner conflict can reach the level of a kind of civil war within the personality.

It is true that unexpected happenings in the outside world can dislodge the most mature person from her place of inner peace and control. The true measure of maturity is the speed in which an individual is able to reestablish inner-core stability through exertion of will. However, when we habitually entertain victim-thoughts about past incidents, we misuse the inner creative-prerogative, and such a self-indulgent habit is difficult to overcome.

Grievances That Bar the Way

The most common causes for repetitive inner conflict are resentments against various people, the past and present players in our lives. Clusters of resentments, buried below the surface, block us from connecting fully to what is good, beautiful, and true. Resentments do this by placing various individuals between us and our MetaValues core. The harm that harbored or "stuffed" grievances do to us cannot be exaggerated. Whether they are justified or not, the results are equally devastating.

In my case, I was one of the lucky ones whom apparently coincidental circumstances saved from a self-created psychic torture chamber. (How this happened is not important to the issue at hand. I share this personal story in the Epilogue of this book.) Over the years, I have learned that many, many people are not so fortunate as I was. So I developed a technique to help them.

You may believe you carry no destructive resentments. Even so, I suggest that you do the exercise that follows. I used a form of it years ago and discovered I had countless unresolved grievances toward a large number of people. Yet, I had no idea that they were there. It is easy to see the need for a clear vision or mission to keep us from being distracted by the petty nonsense and the more wanton evils of the world around us. We can agree with the concept of not taking ourselves too seriously. Clearly, these attitudes are good protection against creating new resentments. But what of the mysterious domain of the subconscious and our collection of long-harbored grievances?

Old, buried grievances are like computer viruses. They operate beneath the surface and constantly play havoc with our thinking efficiency. The process I recommend is similar to one I did in a group therapy session years ago. I was given a yellow tablet and asked to write down the names of all the people I could think of who had harmed me over the years. I had expected that, when finished, my list would fill a page or so with handwritten resentments. Many pages later, I began to grasp the reason I was angry most of the time. An untold number of resentments emerged, beginning with childhood and continuing through adolescence and adult life.

However, there are people reading these pages who need help today, at this very moment. Is it possible to evoke the healing power of MetaValues to heal major grievances by some process or technique now? I believe it is. I thought long and hard about the prolonged healing experience I went through. I became convinced, over time, that although there is a need to acknowledge our resentments against individuals and to seek the healing of those resentments, there is no need to dig and probe into the subconscious and replay episodes of pain and failure. The gateway to joy and freedom may lie in a different direction.

The power of the MetaValues connection will do a vastly more efficient and comprehensive clean-up job than we could by rearranging things in the basement of the subconscious. You don't defeat negative energy by fighting it; confrontation makes it stronger. Negative energy is crowded out and dissolved by the power of a higher concept.

Resentments Are People Perception Problems

We cannot rationally hold resentments against an inanimate object or an abstract incident; our serious grievances are focused against individuals. While we may have myriad resentments and untold numbers of specific incidents that set them into motion, the personalities involved in these resentments are far fewer in number. Each personality triggers a reaction in our conscious minds.

Our mental concepts of personalities function in a similar manner to icons on a computer screen. Each icon is an image-concept that can access billions of bytes of information. When personality-icons are activated in the human mind, they may trigger an uncontrolled torrent of deep, unresolved feelings. The key to destroying a negative mental concept, regardless how powerful or entrenched, is to replace it with a vivid positive concept, and to use MetaValues to embellish and strengthen this new notion until it crowds out the old, negative perception. To be powerful enough to prevail in this contest, the new concept must embrace the qualities of Integrity, Caring, and Excellence.

Most of us know of therapies preoccupied with endlessly digging up the most terrible negative images of a patient's past. These have too often proved to be more damaging than healing. The idea that prevailed during much of the last century—that we are helpless puppets of our unconscious minds—at the same time implied that we are not responsible for what we consciously think and do. When it became fashionable to abdicate personal responsibility, a segment of society exchanged what it perceived as the bondage of "religious superstition" for the bondage of a secular high "priesthood" of professional practitioners who are supposed to be endowed with the power to confront and treat the mysterious monsters of the subconscious.

The Logotherapy concepts of Viktor Frankl challenged this idea. Logotherapy proposes that we can reclaim self-respect by exercising our liberating right to assume the role of responsibility—and thus have an important degree of authority—over the inner life. This philosophy takes us out of the dark caverns and secret terrors of the subconscious, where ghosts and skeletons of the past lurk behind every door. It brings us into the sunlit plateaus of the spiritual superconscious where the task of healing is wholesome and renewing.

The process for healing resentments comes in two parts:

- Identification of the Icons of Resentment.
- Healing the wounds.

Identification of the Icons of Resentment

You'll do this in two sessions. During the first, a pen and one or two sheets of paper are required. Make a list of the people you have come to hold grievances against. Write down, in a single sentence or two, why you resent them. Anticipate that this list will be painful and difficult to make. Allow yourself the time necessary, an interval when you can be alone. Leave no one out; be completely honest.

Include any current people whom you believe have been unjust to you. When you've completed the list, secure it in a safe place.

Personal religious beliefs are quite helpful in healing a troubled mind. Recall that Buckminster Fuller decided to do his own thinking about whether a higher power existed or not. Recall that he asked himself whether he had any personal evidence that indicated that there is a higher intelligence operating in the universe. His answer was that his personal experience persuaded him that there is an orderliness of interactive, exceptionless values or principles undergirding the cosmos. Fuller thus drew the conclusion that his most useful purpose should be to convert all experience toward the advantage of others. At times when his life began to go south, he returned to his commitment to what he called a "greater integrity," and then his life miraculously began to work again. I'm repeating this here because authentic personal spiritual convictions are a powerful resource. Search for yours the way Buckminster Fuller did, and use them throughout this healing process.

Set a date for the second part of this process, from one to seven days from the first session. In the meantime, try not to think about it. Allow the unconscious process to work without interference. Remember that the process of healing resentment is a trade-off. You are giving up a great deal when you give up resentment. You are giving up all rights to your victimhood; you can no longer feel sorry for yourself. If the individual you harbor this resentment toward is still in your life, you will no longer have any weapons to make that person feel guilty. You are setting him or her free. In return, you are also free, and you attain a precious prize: a greater measure of authentic self-respect.

For your second session, put your first list on the table in front of you. Take a new sheet of paper and write the list of people again, with no commentary. Consider the names and imagine what these individuals could have been like *if they had been healthy, happy people.* How would they have treated you if they had not been immature or perhaps emotionally impaired? How would they have looked physically? How would they have acted if they had been healthy, fully functional human beings?

It often surprises me that many religious people, who are able to imagine themselves as children of God, forget that they are not an only child. The corollary is inescapable: these people you resent are also children of God; they are your brothers and sisters. Create an image in your mind of them as the innocent, happy children they once were. The important thing is to develop in your mind's eye a positive visual concept of each of them, a compassionate new perception. Take the time to make sure each new mental image is vivid.

Before I engaged in this process, whenever I thought of my alcoholic father, a host of negative images would flood my mind. After the process, I came to recall the kinder things he did and to realize that there were also happier times. I remembered that he sometimes manifested immense courage, and that he sometimes showed traits of integrity and goodness. I recalled how he never gave up, how he always tried to go to work, even when he was terribly poisoned and hung over from drinking. I remembered some days warmed by love, such as the one in which he played catch with me when I was ten years old. I envisioned his own lonely childhood in rural Indiana and wondered what his impoverished family life was like. I began to realize that I could imagine my dad clean, sober, and free of his addiction to alcohol.

Your task in this first part of the process is to establish a few vivid positive images of the people you resent, and drop these images into your unconscious mind. After you complete this imaging process on each personality, begin at the top and review the list. Access, by means of MetaValues, what Fuller called the *higher integrity*, the greater self within. Consider this access to be toward the highest Integrity, the most compassionate Caring, the supreme Excellence, the ultimate Love. Share with this higher source your desire to heal the associated wounds in your inner life.

In each case, call up from your mind the new positive images you created. Ask that all of the constructive factors you have ever associated with this person be unconsciously gathered and used to embellish the new positive images associated with this personality-icon.

Now, take the original list, the one with the comments on it, and destroy it. Burn it if you like. As you do so, imagine the destruction of the counterpart negative images in your subconscious. Make this effort with all the sincerity you can muster. When you have finished, don't think about it or worry whether you've accomplished what you set out to accomplish. The method you have employed is only the beginning. It sets the process into motion. It cannot take the place of maturity and authentic spiritual growth. All you have done so far is provide a foothold of consent, a fulcrum of willingness that will allow the source of MetaValues to do the real work. Now step aside and turn the entire process over to the transcendent energies within.

If you are like most people, you read the previous pages mentally. You did not physically use a tablet and write things down. This is natural. However, I strongly suggest that you return to this exercise at your convenience and actually go through the writing process. Physical actions help embed mental declarations in the brain's software.

Healing the Wounds

The final step requires a sincere desire to clear up every vestige of related negativity in the subconscious mind. It is essential for you to be utterly sincere when you seek the healing of a grievance. If you feel a block, as though something inside of you does not want to let go of a particular resentment, use the technique of being *willing to be willing*. If a grievance has been with you for quite some time, perhaps your subconscious does not want to let go of it. But you are certainly willing to be willing to have it removed. Take charge of the situation by appealing to the higher levels of the unconscious mind in a manner such as this: "I am not able to release this person. Something inside of me is blocking this process. I have no idea what it is. But I am willing to be willing to have this wound healed. Please clear away my reluctance, and help me release this person and, by so doing, free myself."

Once you have made this appeal, turn the resentment over to the unconscious realms and leave it alone. Don't check on it; have faith that the inner cleansing is being done. If any old resentment comes to mind, immediately switch to the new image. Hold the positive image for a few seconds. Then drop it from your mind.

In a month or so, take the remaining list (the one with names only) and go over it. If any negativity remains, redo the appeal-process for that person in the same manner as before. You are holding on to this resentment for some reason. Even a spark of willingness is adequate for MetaValues and your higher self to begin the work. Each sincere appeal to the "greater integrity" is certain to succeed in achieving some degree of improvement in the inner life. Be at least willing to be willing and be persistent, and the door to peace and freedom will be opened for you.

The Benefits of "Defragging" Your Brain

Almost any professional, in virtually any field, knows the value of a powerful computer augmented by the best software and an effective maintenance program. It would be unthinkable for an architect or a designer to jam his computer hard drive with immature war games he enjoyed as a ten-year-old and leave little room for modern programs. It would court disaster to ignore defragging the computer for long periods. Any professional who accepted a performance level of ten or twenty percent from her computer would be soon out of business.

Yet, how much more foolish is it to have been given the most magnificent instrument known to exist in the cosmos and to cripple it? How unthinking is it to occupy the brain with trivia to a point where it is so reduced in effectiveness as to function barely above the level of a cave dweller. And consider that we often consciously program negative data into this wondrous equipment on a daily basis, rendering it unable to receive inspiring and refreshing spiritual energy to drive its noble functions. When we take on responsibility for the inner life, we clear the wasted creative space. Then our mind's capacity to think and create will be vastly expanded.

TAKING ACTION

Resolutions and growth decisions are important only to the degree that they are completed with actions. By doing the process recommended in this chapter, you have set into motion several action-items required to set the stage for your personal MetaValues breakthrough––a whole new way of life. You are not at a resting place, you are poised for action.

Continue to write your own headlines. Continue to practice active respect. Continue to strive to convert all experience to the advantage of others. Continue to monitor the intrusion of resentments and the triggering of victimhood. With the blocks to self-actualization identified and in the process of removal, we are establishing impregnable self-respect and mastery of the inner life. We are ready to explore a whole new concept of reality and the secret of unlocking your creative genius: *MetaThink.*

CHAPTER SIX

MetaThink™ ... a New Concept of Reality

"The culmination of millions of years of evolution has been the development of the human brain. Not only is the human brain aware of its own existence, but through it the universe has begun to know itself. Our minds have become the spearhead of evolution, and the degree in which we progress depends upon the degree to which we make use of this most incredible product of nature—the degree to which we use our intelligence and our consciousness to the full." [43]

PETER RUSSELL
The Brain Book

"I split myself into three people. I know what they look like. One speculates and one criticizes and the third tries to correlate. It usually turns out to be a fight but out of it comes the whole week's work." [44]

JOHN STEINBECK
Journal of a Novel ... The East of Eden Letters

You were born with the legacy of the most prodigious data processor known to humankind. Unfortunately, you were not given comprehensive training nor even an operator's manual on how to use it. For this reason, few people benefit from even a fraction of their brain's capacity. In fact, even though we rely upon our brains constantly, we have no clue how they work.

If I were to ask you your telephone number, you would respond easily. However, if I were to ask you what looked for that number, where it found the number, and how it delivered that number to your conscious mind, you would be at a loss to answer me. Likewise, we admire people who make their living by creating—by writing, drawing, composing, etc.—yet you might be surprised to learn that creative practitioners really don't know how they do what they do. This is also true of kinesthetic geniuses—the basketball player who can sink a three-pointer without touching the rim, or the golf pro who makes an incredibly difficult putt on unfavorable terrain. The brain computes the math for athletes on a level beyond consciousness to calculate factors like distance, force, trajectory, etc., and translate them to precise commands for the muscles. Like the great creators, world-class athletes simply show up and cooperate with a process that no one can fully explain.

John Steinbeck declared that he was "split into three people" during the creative process, because he sensed he was being engaged in a three-dimensional adventure. Likewise, when you are involved in deep thinking about your life or any major problem or important goal, you may sense that you are also getting information from three sources. In this chapter, I will explain why this is so, and how to make this creative process work so effectively that you will astound those who now underestimate you. I will teach you the remarkable technique of *MetaThink™*, and provide powerful methods to balance the information you receive from the resident "scientist" and "visionary" that are hardwired into your brain.

I call this multidimensional mental process MetaThink, because it transcends ordinary thinking. You will be able to understand MetaThink quickly and put it to use immediately in your life. The secret of MetaValues genius is bound up in MetaThink. MetaThink will connect you to inner resources that are beyond your ability to imagine now.

About the time Abraham Maslow was doing his important early work, John F. Kennedy was President of the United States. President Kennedy has often been heralded as a genius, yet he reportedly had an IQ of 119.[45] Even so, in the domain of intellect, Kennedy gracefully held sway over the most impressive minds of his day and generation. Just a month before his fateful trip to Dallas in 1963, Kennedy was asked during his final press conference if he enjoyed being President. He replied that he did and went on to say that the definition of happiness, according to the ancient Greeks, is the "Full use of your powers along the lines of excellence." [46]

In today's world, the demands on a visionary leader are even greater than they were in the days of John F. Kennedy. For this reason, I suggest expanding the ancient Greek definition to be more in accord with my research into the science of MetaValues: The definition of happiness is the full use of your powers along the lines of Integrity, Caring, and Excellence.

The MetaThink concept will be made clear to you in this chapter. I can write this with confidence, because we all have brains that were hardwired to think in three psychic dimensions:

- the dimension of fact, or the way things are;
- the dimension of value, or the way things ought to be;

- the dimension of synthesis, or how best to get from the way things are to the way things ought to be.

Why have you not heard of these three psychic dimensions before? Sadly, because most people are educated by one-dimensional thinkers who train others to be one-dimensional thinkers. Recipients of this one-dimensional education are then compressed into various logic-tight disciplines that inhibit the scope of their thinking. They are thus able to blend comfortably into society and become pure scientists, religious visionaries, or perhaps academics who are dedicated specialists in one particular field. Before I explain in detail how you can overcome this syndrome, I must tell you a story that should be required reading in every university in the world. This allegory illustrates the dangers of restricted, single-dimension thinking. It was written in the nineteenth century by a minister, Reverend Edwin A. Abbott, the headmaster of the City of London School. His strange work has endured for well over a century and is still in print.

Flatland: A Romance of Many Dimensions

Abbott's novel, *Flatland,* is narrated by a square, a citizen of a two-dimensional world as flat as "a vast sheet of paper." The residents of this land move about freely on its surface, unaware of anything existing above or below them. A third dimension (that of height) is inconceivable to them. The status of the residents of Flatland is determined by the number of sides they have. A triangle has the lowest status, a square is a bit higher, a pentagon yet higher, and so on. The highest status of all is that of the Chief Circle, who is the high priest of Flatland.

One night, the square has an amazing dream. He dreams of a primitive land called Lineland, a land of a single dimension. The residents of this land are all lines or points. The king of Lineland is the longest of these lines. All of these poor creatures understand but one dimension, and moving in any direction other than from side to side is beyond their comprehension.

In this dream, the square elects to tell the king of Lineland about Flatland—his homeland of relatively unlimited potentials. But the king believes the square to be demented. A spirited exchange follows, and the square says angrily, "I am a completion of your incomplete self. You are a line, but I am a Line of Lines … and even I, though infinitely superior to you, am of little account to the nobles of Flatland." This is too much for the king and he orders all of his subjects to prepare to attack the mad intruder. Just before the attack is launched, the square is awakened by the sound of the breakfast bell. To his relief, he is back in reality. But the dream seems to be a mysterious precursor to another event that is to take place as the day progresses.

Later that morning, the square is teaching his grandson plane geometry. He explains that the area of a square can be determined by multiplying the measurement of two of its sides. The lad is quite bright and meditates upon this idea. Then he asks: "You have also shown me numbers can be raised to the third power. Does this have any meaning in geometry?" The square patiently explains that a point, by moving to a length of three inches, makes a line of three inches. "This may be represented by a 3," he says. Then he shows how moving the line of three inches parallel with itself for three inches, a square of three inches is formed with an area of nine inches. "This can be represented by 3 to the second power," the square tells the boy. Now the grandson becomes excited. "Well then, what if a square could move parallel to itself somehow? I can't imagine this, but if it could, would it form something that represented 3 to the third power?"

The square seems to have learned nothing from his dream; he is quite intolerant of the boy's ideas. He becomes quite annoyed at the boy's absurd speculation and finally retorts, "If you would talk less nonsense, you would remember more sense. Go to bed!"

As the day wears on, however, the square cannot get the notions of the young lad out of his mind. Suddenly he exclaims aloud, "The boy is a fool!" And then something most remarkable takes place. The square has a visitation. A voice seems to come from nowhere in particular, saying, "The boy is no fool. Three to the third power has an obvious place in geometry!" The voice says that he is a visitor from Spaceland, a land of three dimensions. Just as the square had called himself a "line of lines" when talking to the residents of Lineland, the visitor claims to be a "Circle of Circles"—a sphere.

Yet, the square does not see a sphere. He sees but a strange circle that grows larger and larger and then begins to diminish in size again. The sphere explains that this is caused because he is entering Flatland from above, and as he passes through the plane, the sphere appears as a circle that seems to change in size. But the square finds this idea bizarre and can understand nothing of what is happening. At this point, the sphere decides to give the square a transcendental experience. He causes the square to enter the third dimension. The square is overwhelmed by what he sees. "Either this is madness or it is hell!" the square exclaims. "It is neither," says the sphere. "It is knowledge. It is Three Dimensions. Open your eye once again and try to look steadily."

The square now becomes emotional. He is so exhilarated by this totally new reality that he begins to imagine that there may be even more "spacious space, some more dimensional dimensionality." There may be a land of four, five, or six dimensions, the square speculates. But these ideas annoy the sphere. "I showed you the ultimate reality. There is no land beyond this, no greater dimension. The very idea is inconceivable," the sphere grumbles. But the square will not be dissuaded. He continues to insist with such energy that the infuriated sphere hurls him back into Flatland.

The square now sees a wonderful career before him in which he can tour Flatland and tell everyone what he has seen with his own eye. He begins to proclaim the great Gospel of Three Dimensions (as best he is able, because he can no longer remember exactly what he has seen). The enlightened square attracts the notice of the authorities, who eventually arrest him and bring him to trial. The square is sent to a benevolent retention center that is much like a modern mental ward.

Each year the Chief Circle visits the square. Inevitably, the square cannot resist trying once more to convince the Chief Circle of what he had seen. The circle always reacts in the same way. He turns away sadly and leaves the mad square alone with his bizarre dreams.

An Endless Series of "Flatlands"

The history of humankind could be measured as a series of self-created flatlands of limitation. Europe was long encased in a flatland of fear until Columbus ventured into the unknown and broke the spell. Galileo and Newton each pushed the frontier yet farther—challenging the imaginations of those who sought to preserve the status quo. Then Einstein ventured beyond the stars—and envisioned a cosmos unbounded by Newton's mechanisms, only to be followed by a host of quantum physics scientists who peered into the world of the infinitely small and discovered yet another unfathomable frontier that appears to defy some of Einstein's paradigms of time and space.

Likewise, daring visionaries, artists, poets, and philosophers have challenged the boundaries of their day and generation, and sought to inspire the human mind to new, higher levels of creative discovery. Just as in the allegory of Flatland, the greatest of these innovators have too often been treated with varying degrees of scorn and doubt by those who were invested in the current boundaries of thought. Perhaps the most tragic examples of the Flatland mindset are the billions of prisons of self-limitation and inner conflict that humankind imposes upon itself. Indeed, it would have been immeasurably helpful if we were given an owner's manual along with our brains. If we were, it would be much easier to use them to fuller capacity. What might such a manual reveal to us about the brain's hardwiring?

Your Two Brains

If you had been given an owner's manual for your brain, the first thing it would reveal to you is that you actually have *two* brains. Each brain has its own consciousness and its own perspective of reality. These two hemispheres are connected by a tissue complex containing countless networks of nerves that transmit information between the two brains. The best evidence that the two brains have separate consciousness is the fact that doctors have surgically removed the entire right brain while a patient is fully conscious, talking to the doctor, and unaware of any difference. (Since the brain feels no pain, these operations can be performed while the patient is conscious.) On the other hand, when a left brain has been surgically removed for medical reasons, patients have lost their ability to speak. They remained conscious, thinking people. Their personalities remained virtually intact, although they were unable to communicate verbally.

How do people retain a sense of their own identity after an operation that removes so much of their dual-brain? Where does consciousness reside? Perhaps the real question is: "Where does our *consciousness of consciousness* reside?" All forms of life seem to have some degree of consciousness. But as far as we can tell, only humans are aware that they are aware. For example, a horse in a stable knows that he is very cold on a bitter winter night. But he does not know that he knows that he is cold. Our ability to be conscious of ourselves as perceivers seems to be part of the software of the human brain. This software exists independently of the brain, yet—apparently, at least—it cannot function without it. Viktor Frankl wrote about this transcendent sense of identity. He called it the irreducible essence of self. We can't define this essence, or even contemplate it, *because the observer cannot be the thing observed*. Frankl believed this essence is a key spiritual component of a human being.

The disciplines of science ask, and strive to answer in various ways, questions about *what is* (material reality). Religious visionaries ideally would seek to ask and answer questions about what *ought to be*. And philosophers should properly ask and answer questions about the methods to get from *what is* (material reality) to what *ought to be* (a vision of a better reality). We are learning now that science, religion, and philosophy need each other. They work with maximum effectiveness when they are able to access and relate to information from each other. This notion can best be understood through allegory. Imagine two geniuses standing in front of you. Each is a master of his particular discipline. Each of these brilliant experts carries a map of the Earth. You can see that the two maps are different. "My map is reality!" shouts one. "My map is reality!" shouts the other.

The first gentleman steps forward. "Look! Here are all of the political boundaries of the world, all of the countries, the cities, the populations, the roads. This is what you need to understand the world!" "Nonsense!" shouts the second. "My map shows the topographical features of the Earth, all of the rivers, the mountains, valleys, forests, and elevations. This is the reality of the planet!" Then, a third expert, a philosopher appears. She has copies of both maps on sheets of acetate. She lays them, one upon the other, and puts them before the two men. "This is a synthesis of your ideas, but even this is nowhere near a model of the reality of the world. You should never crystallize your perceptions of reality. Several billion years from now, humankind will begin to grasp not only what reality is, but what it *means*. From the perspective of the human mind, truth is the emerging, evolving reality which we must experience and constantly redefine as we strive to move from what *is* to what *ought to be*."

But one of the geniuses retorts, "How can you presume to know what ought to be?"

"What ought to be is the ultimate expression of the highest MetaValue of all: *Love*," the philosopher replies. "Love is the synthesis of Truth, Beauty, and Goodness. Love, as the desire to do good to others. Such love is a living expression of evolving reality. This presents the true thinker with new challenges when deciding a course of action: *Will this contemplated action work toward the greatest good for all concerned?*"

Unfortunately, the world's leaders have too often failed to listen to their MetaThinkers. In fact, those with a great deal invested in the status quo have even put MetaThinkers to death. But more and more people, especially the youth, are beginning to understand the deeper realities and significance of enlightened values. MetaValues transcend the confines of materialistic science. The necessary renaissance of consciousness will never be achieved within the segmented, logic-tight disciplines of science, nor those of formal theology. The best of each discipline is needed, fully synthesized by MetaValue insights. The application of classic scientific methods alone has too often proven to be inadequate to solve modern problems.

> "*The eye of the material mind perceives a world of factual knowledge; the eye of the spiritualized intellect discerns a world of true values. These two views, synchronized and harmonized, reveal the world of reality, wherein wisdom interprets the phenomena of the universe in terms of progressive personal experience.*" [47]

Our Advisors:
The Scientist, the Visionary, and the Philosopher

The human brain seems to have been designed for MetaThinking *(see Figure Three)*. The left hemisphere of the brain is generally acknowledged as the seat of logical, pragmatic, fact-oriented thinking. It is time-conscious, the word-thinking center of our speech, and can be a wonderful servant in determining what is. The right hemisphere is the seat of creative thinking. It is intuitive, conceptual, and unbound by time. For these reasons, we might say that the left brain is our resident scientist and the right brain is our resident visionary.

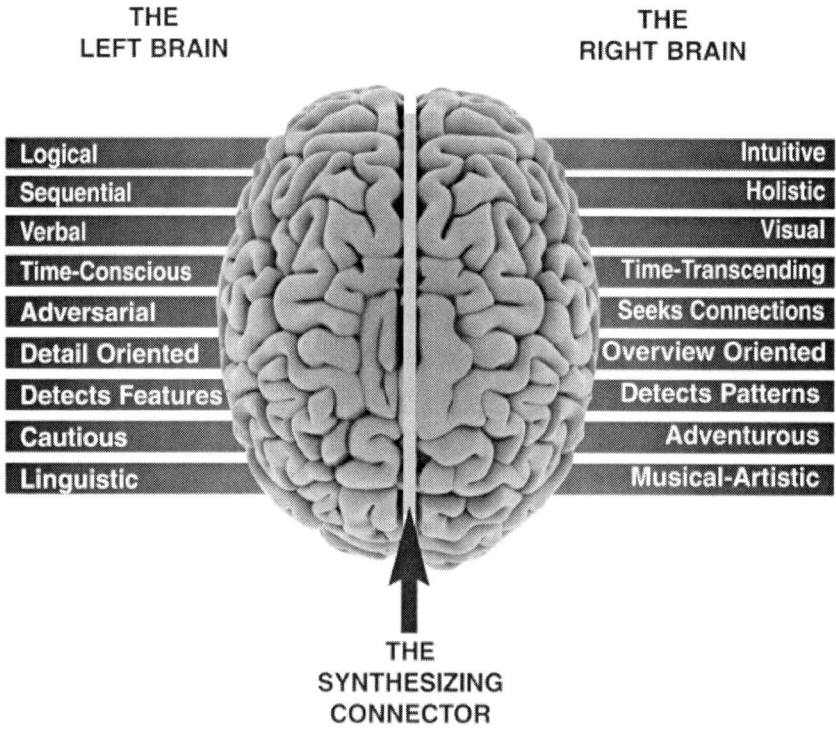

THE
LEFT BRAIN

THE
RIGHT BRAIN

Logical	Intuitive
Sequential	Holistic
Verbal	Visual
Time-Conscious	Time-Transcending
Adversarial	Seeks Connections
Detail Oriented	Overview Oriented
Detects Features	Detects Patterns
Cautious	Adventurous
Linguistic	Musical-Artistic

THE
SYNTHESIZING
CONNECTOR

Figure Three – How Your Brain is Hard-Wired
To Perceive Multidimensional Reality

The two points of view, the scientific and the visionary, are synthesized by the passage of billions of messages back and forth each second between the two hemispheres. We (that is, the essence of inner identity) might be considered to be the resident philosopher, and our task is to oversee this synthesizing process. We can thus determine or define the meaning of what our "two brains" perceive. Here is another way of saying all of this: The left hemisphere gathers information and provides the material fact of what is and the right hemisphere conceptualizes a vision of what could be. There is obviously a gap between what is and what ought to be, and we evaluate the meaning of this gap by synthesizing the two perspectives. Ideally, we should then strive to *take action* and close this gap.

It is upon the vast loom that exists between what is and what should be that we weave our destiny, with threads of thought and action. And, it is in this realm of moral choice where our human will can assert its relative creative freedom.

Most modern specialists can be likened to Flatlanders when they see things in one dimension. Perhaps they are materialists who can only think in terms of material reality—what is. Or they may be dreamers, who can only think in terms of what ought to be, and who are not grounded in reality. Or, worst of all, they may be stuck in the dead center of indecision. Many people simply can't make up their minds.

The MetaThinker transcends the compartments between the essential disciplines. Traditionally, the materialist took pride in power, and the poet reminded him to temper power with compassion. But now things happen too fast. The voices of the poet and the visionary are sometimes ignored. What the world needs now are *leaders* who are MetaThinkers *(see Figure Four)*.

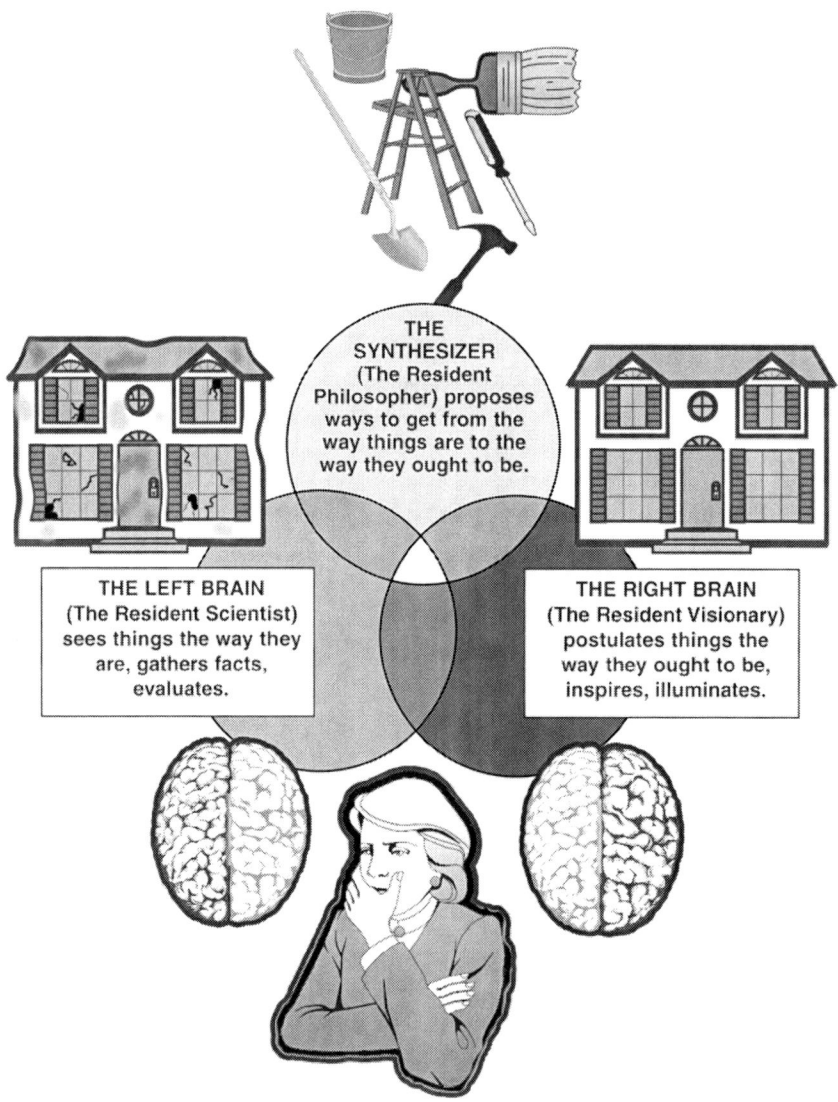

Figure Four – The MetaThinker

However, though MetaThink is a necessary element to a safe, progressive world, it is not the whole answer. With information coming from two brains, how can we be certain we are making the right decision? No wonder Steinbeck likened his creative work to a fight. Even if we complete our decision by acting it out, how can we be assured we are doing the right thing?

The Shortest Route and the Fastest Path

We must return once more to Buckminster Fuller for the most powerful formula for right action: "Convert all experience to the highest advantage of others." This is a daring, almost counterintuitive concept. Yet Fuller declared that when he committed to making it his purpose to serve others by helping abet their "inclusion" into the "design of the universe," his life altered beyond recognition. He said he "chickened" many times, and when he did, everything went wrong. Only when he returned to his commitment did things begin to work again.

It took me years to understand the depth of Fuller's statement. He was saying that when he worked toward helping others achieve harmony with the plan of the universe, things fell into place for him. The universe seemed to rush to his assistance. But when he deviated from his focus on unselfish service, he became out of sync with the plan of the universe and things began to go wrong. Unselfish service reaches the highest levels of power and effectiveness when it results in the actualization of something good, beautiful, and true. Some rare individuals who may have never heard of MetaValues strive to do this intuitively. For most of us, this path requires a great deal of conscious effort.

It is reasonable to assert that we live in a materialistic world too often dominated by left-brain thinkers. In most individuals, the left brain, being the seat of language, easily dominates the right. IQ tests were traditionally weighted toward the ability to demonstrate skill in understanding and using language. You may have noted that word-experts tell us what to think, what movies and plays to attend, and what books to read. Word-people even tell us which works of art are of importance and which are not. Too often, the general public passively accepts aggressive word-people as authorities. MetaThink insists we think for ourselves, that we challenge the broad assumptions of both those who presume to tell us the way things are and those who fancy that they know the way things ought to be. Recall Buckminster Fuller's breakthrough was set into motion when he decided to start thinking for himself. MetaThink is based upon the premise that MetaValues provide an inner compass that points toward right action and, once you are in motion, keeps the wheels from falling off.

So, exactly what is the practical application for MetaThink? How can you put MetaThink to work for you this very day and begin to revolutionize your life? First, understand the three cardinal principles of applying MetaThink:

- **The work is important, the self is not**. Of all the pitfalls in personal growth, the most tempting and dangerous is pride. Personal ego is like a clerk residing in the conscious realm of the mind. If the clerk is not humble and willing to acknowledge that the immense spectrum of mental activities that takes place is beyond the scope of his consciousness, trouble ensues. The ego begins to take credit for everything. The clerk begins to imagine that he is running the entire enterprise. In fact, his greatest power is his ability to allow the process or shut it off. Every professional athlete or artist knows that if the conscious mind begins to take over and attempts to direct things, the three-pointer hits the rim and the piano concerto loses its nuanced depth and richness.

When you synthesize and harmonize both sides of your brain's output, you more fully employ the enormous powers of the mind. You thus tap into resources of remarkable magnitude. Yet, just as you have no idea how you bring your phone number into the field of consciousness, you will never have much conscious understanding of how MetaThink works. Very little of the mind's work is conscious. The most important conscious acts you will participate in are the choices you will make. Without your consent, nothing happens. But once you choose to flick the switch, you are connected to an immense network that will serve you with elegance and precision. All you need do is show up and push the right button.

Much the same thing happens when you power up your computer. Until you push the power button, it is simply a big box of cold possibilities. But once you give consent and act on your decision to use your computer and log on to the Internet, it comes to life. Incalculable gigabytes of information are at your fingertips. You are suddenly connected to virtually any spot on the planet. If you are able to install and master the right software, you can make wonderful graphics that would have taken a professional illustrator days and even weeks to complete a few decades ago. Yet, think about it: although you have mastered the technique of pushing the right buttons, do you really know what is taking place? Can you really take credit for much more than knowing what buttons to push? And, if the buttons fail to work, do you know how to fix the computer?

Avoid the pitfalls of pride and self-aggrandizement by remembering this mantra: *The work is important, the self is not.*

▪ **Maintain the vision of what you want, that which ought to be.** You have heard of the importance of vision before. However, in the left-brain world in which we live, few people understand the life-altering significance of maintaining a vision. The operative word is maintaining. It is not enough to have a splendid vision. Usually, once the work begins, the vision is the first thing lost and the left brain takes over. Our conscious mind becomes mired in concern about obstacles and fear of failure.

Walt Disney achieved the creative successes he did because he understood this principle. Michael Vance tells us that Disney always used six humans and one accountant on every creative team. By this, Vance meant that Disney used six right-brain visionaries and one materially-grounded left-brainer. He understood that very few people are able to MetaThink—to integrate an inspiring vision with practical realities—and create a master plan. Disney also knew that, although the appropriate amount of left-brain practical insight will help keep the project financially and materially on track, a little practicality goes a long way. Left-brainers tend to aggressively dominate teams, and they must be outnumbered or the team effort may grind to a halt. John F. Kennedy defined the exquisite tension between materialistic thinking and visionary insight in this way:

> *"When power leads man towards arrogance, poetry reminds him of his limitations. When power narrows the areas of man's concern, poetry reminds him of the richness and diversity of his existence. When power corrupts, poetry cleanses. For art establishes the basic*

human truth which must serve as the touchstone of our judgment." [48]

Most of us fail to achieve our dreams because we let our left brains sabotage our efforts with thoughts of fear and admonitions toward safety. Growth choices cannot be made and carried out if we are too self-concerned and dominated by fear. At the first sign of discomfort or danger, we will run back to our comfort zone. Once fear takes over, the result is an abrupt disconnect. The network goes down and the circuits go dark. Hence, our second requisite for MetaThink: *Maintain the vision of what you want, that which ought to be.* You must believe in your vision, you must have faith in its promise. You must be armed against the Jonah Complex by means of an impregnable self-respect.

▪ **Measure all of your ought-to-be's with the benchmark of MetaValues—Truth, Beauty, and Goodness actionized as Integrity, Excellence, and Caring.** The triumph of the human spirit is assured—beyond all doubt and in spite of any apparent circumstances—when it wills its own wholehearted, unconditional commitment to be personally guided and actualized by the MetaValues of Truth, Beauty, and Goodness. We can, in the manner of Flatland, see this statement on one level as a mere platitude. Or, we can imagine the implications of it on higher levels of reality. If we really believed these words to be ultimately true, how would we act? What would we do this very day? How could we be afraid? The still, small voice within will not give us peace until we begin moving in the direction of our dreams—regardless of how vague and undefined these dreams may be at this moment. Your role in this process is simply to show up, turn on the power, and follow your inner, intuitive directions.

Our action-objective is to start the conscious cultivation of your creative power in new and positive ways. Creativity is the key to freedom and self-actualization. Maslow conjectured that when we discuss creativity and self-actualization, we may be talking about the same thing. The Self-Actualizer deliberately *consults* the resident visionary (the right brain) more often and more robustly than the non-actualizer. The Self-Actualizer *acts* upon the advice of the resident visionary with greater confidence and focus. *Self-actualization itself may simply be the capturing of an ought-to-be vision and the relentless devotion to its fruition.*

Begin to capture the visions of your right brain. Set aside time——perhaps a half hour——every day to spend with your muse, your resident visionary. She is always eager to provide good ideas, and occasionally great visions. We are usually too busy, too occupied with problems and concerns to listen. During this half hour, you are stepping into the "eye of the hurricane," where there is always total calm. Surely no one has ever been confronted with greater burdens than George Washington during the dark days of the Revolutionary War. He would give orders that he was not to be disturbed at certain times, and this is when he renewed his inner strength. Set aside a half hour tomorrow to begin the process of consulting with your resident visionary. During this period, strive to think in pictures, not words.

Capture these creative ideas by commanding your left brain to record them in writing. Carry a small notebook and record creative ideas when they come through at odd times during the day. Cultivate this new partnership with your resident visionary. Genuine eurekas are rare and could come at any time. When they do, you just won the lottery. Those ought-to-be's have tremendous power. They preexist somewhere, waiting to be discovered and actualized by a human mind. An individual's single most important lifetime decision is the choice of what primary idea will use him. Somewhere out there is a significant ought-to-be with your name on it. Your MetaValues breakthrough will be set into motion when you yield to it. Harry Emerson Fosdick, who was the renowned minister of New York's Riverside Church for decades, wrote of such ought-to-be's, "The greatest hour in a man's life is when he turns the corner of a street and turns into a new idea. That is certainly the greatest hour of many a youth's life, especially if, as the youth faces that idea or cause, there rises in him the invincible conviction that he belongs to it." [49]

Make no mistake: we are all being used by ideas all the time. For too many of us, these ideas are limiting beliefs that someone else made up, notions we have assumed were true and we have adopted. For the fortunate few, the Buckminster Fullers and the Marva Collinses, the ideas that used them were ought-to-be's upon which their names were emblazoned. Remember that your supreme ought-to-be needs you as much as you need it. Even the most wonderful concept has no temporal power until it finds a human channel to manifest it. Until then, it is but a potential. But your great vision will simply fade into oblivion if you do not act upon it. The first step is to record it. Then begin to embellish it.

The Drift Delusion. Most people suffer from what I call the *Drift Delusion.* They are as yet without their marvelous, vivid dream of something that ought to be. Perhaps you also believe that, one glorious morning, God will whisper your momentous task into your ear. And perhaps this will happen. But in the meantime, *what are you becoming?* Will you be ready when this realization takes place?

What are you to do in the meantime? As Robert H. Schuller of California's Crystal Cathedral once pointed out, even God cannot steer a parked car. Surely, there must be a way to fill the unforgiving minute with meaning and purpose. Surely, there is a way to move in the general direction of our dreams—even when we cannot see the ultimate destination. Indeed, there is.

"Trust only movement," declared Alfred Adler. He knew that the attitude of holding back and avoiding commitment prevents you from interacting with the very dynamics that are necessary to help you discover your dream. The Drift Delusion is the strategy of procrastination and ease-seeking. It is the fatal error of believing you can keep your talent, enthusiasm, and wholehearted commitment on hold until you discover what it is you really want to do. This idea is the opium of mediocrity.

- **The Next-Step Strategy.** The antidote for the Drift Delusion is the *Next-Step Strategy.* It is based upon this premise: Although few of us can articulate the ultimate vision or purpose for our lives, we all know what our next step should be. Your next step is the thing you think about now and then, but have failed to act upon. It may be a modest step, such as cleaning that workroom and beginning in earnest to prepare for your new career as a writer. It may be signing up to take those classes you keep thinking about. Or making that contact you fear may reject you. The important thing is movement in the direction of your dreams. However slight, this movement awakens forces around you that are poised and anxious to aid you. The Next-Step Strategy isn't something you do once and forget. You must use it daily. You must develop the habit of confronting your fears and taking action each day.

TAKING ACTION

Do the process of capturing ideas, embellishing them, and planning next steps for several days before going on to chapter seven. Then we will take the visualization process to another level. Having a magnificent data processor––the human brain––and knowing something about how it works is important, but not enough. The Internet exponentially multiplied the power of the computer. The MetaValues connection achieves even more for the mind if we acquire the right visualization software, install it, and learn to master it. In our next chapter, you will learn about the software that world-class performers employ and how to obtain it and put it to work in your life.

CHAPTER SEVEN
Vision and the Will-to-Excellence

"Yet we have all experienced times when, instead of being buffeted by anonymous forces, we do feel in control of our actions, masters of our own fate. On the rare occasions that it happens, we feel a sense of exhilaration, a deep sense of enjoyment that is long cherished and that becomes a landmark in memory for what life should be like." [50]

MIHALY CSIKSZENTMIHALYI
FLOW, The Psychology of Optimal Experience

"We have now become much less conscious of everything other than the matter-at-hand … When you are totally absorbed in non-self, you tend to become less conscious of yourself, less self-aware. You are less apt to be observing yourself like a spectator or a critic … All these characteristics are part of self-forgetfulness and audience-forgetfulness. Absorption casts out fear." [51]

ABRAHAM MASLOW
The Farther Reaches of Human Nature

Charles Garfield wondered how he ever got into this predicament. He looked down at his body; it was hooked up with dozens of probes and wires. The wires led to a complex of machines that were monitoring his pulse, temperature, brain waves, and other physiological activities. The Soviet psychologists and sports physiologists who surrounded him were busy taking notes, whispering among themselves, and occasionally observing him.[52]

The year was 1979. Garfield, an American Olympic weightlifting coach, had been lecturing in Milan. After his talks, he began to have conversations with a group of Soviet Union experts in athletic performance who contested many of Garfield's training ideas. Several days of good-natured debate followed. During one of these late-night discussions, Garfield implied that the only reason the Russian Block athletes had achieved such astounding results in competition was that they used drugs. This accusation offended the Soviet experts. They insisted that Garfield accompany them to a gym, where they promised they would reveal their secrets of world-class performance.

It was very late, and the Soviets had to pull strings to get someone to open the training facility. Once inside, they carefully unpacked a host of impressive instruments and hooked Garfield up to them. Then they began to interview Garfield intensely, making computations, and taking notes. *How often did Garfield work out with weights?* Garfield replied that he had not done any important exercise for eight years. Back then, at his peak, he had bench-pressed 365 pounds. *How much did Garfield think he could bench-press now?* Garfield suggested that he might be able to do 300 pounds, certainly no more than that. *How long did he think it would take him to work up to 365 pounds again?* Garfield guessed it would take about nine months to a year to reach his old record.

Then, at the urging of the trainers, Garfield attempted a 300-pound bench-press. It was very difficult; he barely made the lift. Now the Soviets began to make calculations and measurements again, even taking a blood test. At last, they announced that they were ready to complete their demonstration.

Garfield sat upon a bench, still wired to the network of monitors. He was told to loosen up, to lie back, and to relax. The Soviet scientists talked him into drifting into a deeper and deeper state of relaxation. Although completely awake and alert, in time Garfield felt more at ease than he ever had in his life. The Soviets suggested his arms were growing warm and heavy. Garfield began to feel a remarkable tingle throughout his body. After forty minutes in a deep, meditative, receptive state, the trainers gently suggested that he sit up and contemplate the barbell before him. They had loaded it to 365 pounds––sixty-five pounds more than the weight he had barely lifted before!

"Imagine yourself approaching the bar with utter confidence," a trainer whispered in his ear. "See yourself lying down and actually pressing the weight. In your mind you must feel the cold bar, the rough knurled area for gripping; hear the weights rattling; hear your own breathing." The suggestion caused an immediate anxiety reaction from Garfield that sent the monitor readings into orbit. But the Soviet trainers were quietly confident. They continually assured him of his power. They urged him to see himself lifting the bar.

Their monologue began to crowd out and replace the Will-to-Fail conversation that had been going on in Garfield's mind. They told him to zoom in and out of the positive visual images that were playing in his mind; to view himself from above, from the side; to see his hands up close. Repeatedly, they went through the visualization process, asking him to imagine how his muscles would feel when he completed the lift. Garfield wrote about the astounding transformation that began to take place:

> *"Surprisingly, everything began to come together for me … The imagery now imprinted in my mind began to guide my physical movements. Slowly and patiently, their voices sure yet gentle, the Soviets led me through the lift. I became convinced I could do it. The world around me seemed to fade, giving way to self-confidence, belief in myself, and then to deliberate action."* [53]

When the Soviet experts saw that Garfield had reached the moment of peak physical and mental resonance, they quickly unhooked him from the equipment. Garfield moved in, positioned himself, and promptly lifted the weight.

Charles Garfield never forgot the experience. He began to develop new ideas about the possibilities of what he termed Peak Performance and to apply them to American Olympic athletes, with impressive results. He began to write books and give lectures on the untapped potential of all Americans, not just athletes. He saw a definite overlap between the work of the Russian and American psychologists, especially Abraham Maslow. Garfield wrote:

> *" … there is now not a shadow of a doubt in my mind that the Soviets have long been aware of the work of the American psychologist Abraham Maslow and of his exploration of what he called 'peak experiences' and the emotional foundations that accompany such moments."* [54]

It is perhaps surprising that the Russians, under the banner of materialistic Communism, made the original studies that led to Garfield's Peak Performance concept. But the Russians were, above all, pragmatic. After World War II, they began to investigate the people who had survived the Nazi death camps. Casualties due to starvation and disease were extremely high among the inmates who were not sentenced to gas chambers. The Russians wanted to know why some people were able to withstand the horror and deprivation of the concentration camps while others were not.

The Soviets learned that certain individuals manifested inner reserves that made them far more capable of surviving than the average person. These individuals were able to extend their endurance and abilities far beyond the normal limits. The Russians became intrigued by this inner power of self to assert the will against hopeless odds. They began to apply the principles they learned from death camp survivors to the training of dancers, musicians, athletes, and other performers. They even applied the ideas to their training of cosmonauts in the space program. However, it is important to note that the Soviet top performance programs were limited to feats of skill alone; there was no spiritual component such as MetaValues in their training. The emotional foundations that accompany those peak experiences and superlative performances can be achieved by athletes and other performers without consciousness of MetaValues. But they cannot be sustained. Some of the most wonderful Soviet performers were bitterly unhappy and led tragic lives.

The Living Software of Success

Garfield's experience in Milan was a natural, repeatable scientific experiment. It was not hocus-pocus, but rather a demonstration of the importance of installing the right software before attempting a peak performance. Think about it. Nothing had materially changed in Garfield. He had exactly the same muscle structure and mental capacity when he completed the lift as he had when he was certain it was impossible. The Soviets had succeeded in temporarily crowding out Garfield's assumptions about his abilities by activating new faith and confidence. His experience vividly demonstrated that our ability to do directly correlates with the belief that we can do. Garfield's feat was a valuable demonstration that a vivid state of mind of anticipated success is overwhelmingly powerful.

But is this something you and I can aspire to? Can these lessons be applied to our own challenges? Later, after researching over 1,500 peak performers over a period of eighteen years, Charles Garfield concluded that any of us can learn the basic skills that exceptional performers have. Today, as never before in human history, we are challenged to manage change and embrace the future. Just as the athletes and astronauts of the last century, we must leave behind the limiting beliefs that keep us in our comfort zones. Garfield wrote:

> *"We see it, again and again, in peak performers— leaving what is 'known' about human limitations, leaving notions of which of us can be peak performers, leaving old structures of organization, leaving beliefs that have served us well and now hold us back … We will have to be peak performers to accommodate the changes that await us."* [55]

We all want to be peak performers. But there are no easy shortcuts. Self-actualization is about more than achieving a great performance. Or even a series of great performances. Self-actualization is about embracing the whole of the life experience to its fullest. It is about spending more and more time doing things you really want to do; being places you really want to be; developing relationships with the people you really want to be with—and all of these things in concert with a devotion to a cause that is greater than self. In the words of self-empowerment expert Anthony Robbins, "Getting what you want is not the purpose of life. Getting what you want will not make you happy. What will make you incredibly happy is becoming what you need to be." [56]

MetaThink Software for Peak Performance

To become what we need to be and meet the enormous multitasking challenges of this millennium, we will revisit Garfield's ideas and systematically complement them with Dr. Maslow's concept of MetaValues. Athletes and performers have reached remarkable levels of achievement using only a portion of Maslow's self-actualizing concept. Imagine what we could accomplish by integrating the complete theory—especially his MetaValues discoveries.

All of us are being called. As Garfield pointed out, we are not simply called to do new things; we are called to be our new selves. MetaValues provide the constant renewal, the constant flow of inspiration, energy, and will to actualize such a transformation. But your great transformation will not be set into motion until you make the commitment to methodically and resolutely replace your old mental software with dynamic new programs. You must be truly ready to change the way you think. Rather than dwelling on difficulties and problems, begin to focus on possibilities that ought to be, and everything else will follow.

A purely selfish vision is very different from something that ought to be. Non-actualizers are needy people, focused upon themselves and the acquirement of something (material or emotional) that they lack or imagine they lack. This is what we call a deficiency need, not an ought-to-be. However, when a vision focuses away from self and suggests bringing something true, beautiful, and good into being for the benefit of humankind, it could well be an ought-to-be. If the means you choose to do this are appropriate and the timing is right, nothing can stop you.

The single most powerful mental software needed for MetaValues transformation has already been "factory installed" for you. It will be activated the instant you visualize a possibility that ought to be. If you decide to actualize this vision, you will feel the power of this mental software begin to focus and energize your mind. If you are one of the fortunate few who complete your decision by acting on it, the factory-installed program will become fully activated. Provided you reach this action level, the ought-to-be you visualized will take on a life of its own. Instead of pushing yourself to work on your project, you will find yourself being pulled along with it. And what a ride it will be.

However, unlike an athletic or stage performance, life is not a single mega-challenge, nor even a series of such challenges. It is a continuous, seamless process that is intended to engage you every second of every day. How do we achieve the state of mind that operates with grace, power, and poise at all times so we can face the big things and the little things with precisely the same degree of confidence and love? Can we approach a humdrum day with the same balance of poise, passion, and focus that Garfield achieved when he approached that 365-pound barbell? Can we sustain this sense of power and purpose? We can, and I will show you how.

In the last chapter, we examined the technique of MetaThink and learned how the basic hardwiring of the brain works. Now we will methodically choose and install the software that will energize the brain and inspire us to engage life as never before. There is a specific procedure to engage this process. Garfield and Maslow agreed that the difference between self-actualizing performers and ordinary people is much less than most of us believe. But the small difference has tremendous leverage and will make a huge difference in performance.

Before we start, a few final words of advice. Physical well-being depends upon the proper balance of three key factors: adequate sleep and relaxation, a regular exercise program, and proper nutrition. Likewise, mental well-being depends upon a grasp and acceptance of the reality of what is, an optimistic and inspiring vision of what ought to be, and the ability to balance and integrate these and all related factors. When a mind achieves perfect poise and the body is properly cared for, the MetaValues process is easiest to engage and maintain. When the physical, mental, and spiritual powers of an individual are in "triune harmony" and reasonable balance, then the MetaValues breakthrough can safely open a new world of extravagant possibilities for your consideration and growth choices.

Recall the Soviets took Garfield through four simple stages before he was called upon to perform. No world-class performer would think of beginning a performance without a warm-up period. We are all called upon to strut our stuff each day, no less than great athletes and world-class performers. But so many people rush out each day without proper preparation, plunging into their tasks, fretting and worrying and bumbling through. It doesn't have to be that way. We can prepare for the challenges of the day by warming up as the top professionals do for their performances. If you followed my advice in the previous chapter, you have already begun this daily warm-up process. You have set aside a half hour and begun to consciously cultivate the creative visionary power of the right brain. Now we are going to reach for another level.

Read the following material completely before attempting the process. Then set aside a time when you can have at least an hour to devote to this experiment.

TAKING ACTION

1. Setting the Stage: the *Know Thyself* Review

The Soviets first did an intensive interrogation of Charles Garfield. They needed to know the reality of his current mindset. As he answered their questions, he also informed himself about his perceived limitations at that exact moment in time. We begin our introspection in a similar way, with our "resident scientist" gathering data about our deepest convictions. Record your answers to the following *Know Thyself* review.

As works in progress, we are all engaged in a process of becoming, a process that constitutes what we call life. Philosophers often pose three questions: *Who am I? Where did I come from?* and *Where am I going?* Socrates expressed the ultimate challenge in two immortal words: *Know thyself.* However, I have come to believe that the bottom-line issue is not these unanswerable questions.

Rather, it is an inquiry we can answer: *What am I becoming?* This is a question that cannot be avoided. Even if we do not consciously ask it, a voice within—on some level—relentlessly implores it of us. Being something special or having important status is not enough. Being able to leap tall buildings with a single bound is not enough. Full use of your powers along the lines of Excellence is not enough. The yardstick for you as a self-actualizing individual of this millennium is the full use of your powers along the lines of Integrity, Excellence, and Caring.

So answer this question: What am I becoming?

Then answer these others:

- **Am I on the right bus?** Fortunately, we are all blessed with a factory-installed, infallible warning system that gives off alarms when we are on the wrong bus and in the company of the wrong people. Unfortunately, we too often ignore it. Pick your bus and your companions with great care. Above all, heed your internal alarm system. Once you are on the right bus, you will know it. The interior lights will come on, the scenery will become gorgeous and fragrant, and you will be surrounded by kindred spirits who respect, love, and support you. The ride will be so much more effortless and fun.

- **How can I fill each unforgiving minute with meaning?** Life was not intended to be a few high points separated by long stretches of meaningless activity. We have an infallible meaningful-activity gauge within that tells us when life is without meaning. Everything turns dreary, stifling, and boring. These are the characteristics of the dead center of indecision. It is a signal that we are drifting, shrinking back from deciding and acting. Yet most people accept a dull sense of boredom and meaninglessness as an inevitable part of life. It is not. It is the waste of life, and causes an untold dissipation of time. The time is now. This is the day that surpasses all other days.

- **Am I committed to a lifetime philosophy of continuous improvement, and where am I on this road?** It would be nice if we could set the controls, go on automatic pilot, and drift off to sleep. In fact, the vast majority of people virtually live in this state of tedious drift. Challenging visions come into their minds, only to gradually fade away. Next-step activities are put off interminably. Indeed, the great tragedy of most lives is not that they are lived in an evil way, but rather that they are lived at an intensity that is a tiny fraction of their possibilities. However, you are one of the fortunate few. You are growing in character each day. Each failure only strengthens your resolve. Perhaps you have not fully defined your grand goal in life as yet, but you can faintly see its broad outlines. And you are willing to take the next steps and move in the direction of your dreams. You understand the need to fill the unforgiving minute with meaning, you are willing to act in the now. You strive for a sense of motion, of life, of movement. You still have a long way to go, yet you have made marvelous progress. However, we cannot measure our progress while we are in a frenzy of activity. The purposeful, exceptional life must be methodically and continuously examined. Course corrections must be made. You can't do these things unless you constantly monitor where you are.

2. The Relaxation Process

Reading the material above is like reading the manual of a computer program. Good ideas, but nothing happens until the software is installed. Even then, productivity depends upon the ability of the operator to establish ownership as well as obtain the necessary daily upgrades of the software. This is accomplished exactly as Garfield's lift was accomplished, by first preparing the mind with a combination of relaxation and focus. Relaxation establishes the capacity to receive MetaValues input; focus enables the mind to connect with the spiritual essence within. To do this, you must invest a reasonable amount of time. Before you begin each day, set aside a half hour or so that is devoted to replacing weakness with strength, fear with courage, and purely selfish motives with the ought-to-be's of the universe.

When you conduct these processes daily, they establish strength-giving and value-receptive habits. These build character, and exceptional character is what drives self-actualization. The regular practice of engaging in this kind of preparation is time-consuming at first. But eventually it becomes time-saving as well as refreshing. As more and more complex demands are made upon us, it becomes critical to conserve and cultivate your spiritual energies.

Get into a comfortable position and relax the body. Tense each muscle group and relax it. Begin at your feet and go through the entire body. Recall that it took Garfield forty minutes to transcend an extremely tense state of mind and reach optimum relaxation. Eventually, you can reach the necessary level of relaxation in a few minutes. Once you have emptied the mind and calmed the body, you are ready to concentrate on the goal to connect with your highest vision of personal excellence and to exchange doubt for faith, fear decisions for growth decisions, and tentativeness for positive action.

3. The Reprogramming Process

Recall that Garfield's mind was filled with negative inner talk when the Soviets loaded up the barbell with his record lift. The Soviets replaced Garfield's assumptions about his abilities by activating new faith and confidence. They did this by flooding his mind with realistic, positive images of success. The Soviets knew these visions were realistic based upon the scientific measurements they made. Remember the maxim: The power to do can only be achieved by the belief that one can do.

Dispel negative self-talk. Nothing devastates confidence more effectively than negative self-talk. Recall the lesson of Gene Tunney: Every contest is won or lost before it is fought. Rehearse success. In your mind's eye, see yourself meeting challenges with grace and power, and operating from an inner core of peace.

Never begin the day's work until you acquire the attitude of the peak performer; failure to do this is not an option. Never begin the day until you have written your own headlines. Take what time you need to create this personal software of success. You have been underestimated. And you have underestimated yourself. What you have achieved is good, but it is only the overture to the wonderful things you are yet to accomplish. Each day, ask and answer the question: *What am I becoming?* Each day, resolve to acquire the state of mind that Garfield had when he made that "impossible" barbell lift. To do this, you need to download the day's software of success.

4. The Performance

Review and evaluate yesterday's performance. First, what did you do right? What did you accomplish? What new contacts were made, what progress, what problems solved? Next, what do you need to improve? What would you have done differently yesterday if you had not been afraid? What can you do today that you were afraid to do yesterday?

5. Use the Pareto Principle

Everyone has a to-do list. But nearly everyone begins the day without time-framing each item and prioritizing them. People who have adopted the following method report important leaps in productivity. The driving notion behind the Pareto Principle is: 80% of what we do produces 20% of the results. Likewise, 20% of what we do generates 80% of the results. To apply the Pareto Principle, take a tablet and make two columns. Label one column "80s" and the other "20s." Using your intuition, sort all the items on your master list of things to do. The things that you intuitively know are 80% producers are naturally the most important, and require further sorting.

Next, time-frame the 80% productive items. How long do you estimate it will take to complete each one? *This step is critical.* You will likely be surprised to note that many of your 80s items will take only five or ten minutes to complete. Finally, prioritize your 80s list. Put those five- and ten-minute 80s items at the top of your list. (These are most often phone calls or communications you have been putting off.) Once your list of 80s is made, time-framed, and prioritized, barring emergencies, the sequence must be virtually nonnegotiable. Now you are ready for anything. Emergencies and interruptions will occur, of course. But once they are handled, return to your 80s list. If you finish with all your 80s, you can start on your 20s.

One final note on emergencies. Most of them happen because you are not doing the routine things you need to do on a regular basis. For example, answering e-mails, paying bills, sorting and attending to snail mail, etc. All these must be done daily and on a routine basis. For this reason, some people like to designate routine items with an "R" and get them out of the way first.

You do not have to follow these outlines for a daily warm-up exactly. What we are striving to achieve is a state of mind in which failure is not an option. Do what works for you. If you have gone through this process with this state-of-mind resolve, you have set the stage. You have done your part. You showed up, you cleared the deck. Now move, begin, and your courage will evoke the "genius, power, and magic" of MetaValues. This will accomplish what ought to be.

I suggest that you do not go on to the next chapter until you have practiced this process for several days.

When you complete the next chapter, you will become one of the small group of individuals who have clearly defined their mission in life. You will have created a working ought-to-be vision that will illuminate and enrich each day of your life with new meaning and purpose.

CHAPTER EIGHT
Toward Full Use of Your Powers

"What is disclosed to consciousness [from without] is something that is; however, what is revealed to conscience [from within] is ... something that ought to be. What merely ought to be is not real, but is something to make real; ... (although in a higher, ethical sense, such a possibility again represents a necessity) ... To anticipate what is not yet, but is to be made real, conscience must be based on intuition ... But is not conscience in this respect analogous to love? ... both love and conscience have to do with something, or someone, absolutely unique." [57]

VIKTOR FRANKL
Man's Search for Ultimate Meaning

"This [Self-Actualizer's] list of described characteristics of reality, of the world, seen at certain times, is just about the same as what have been called the eternal values ... the old familiar trinity of truth, beauty, and goodness ... These characteristics are what the great religionists and philosophers have valued, and this is practically the same list that most serious thinkers of mankind have agreed upon as the ultimate or highest value of life ... The world ... which is described and perceived becomes the same as the world which is valued and wished for. The world which is becomes the world which ought to

be. That which ought to be has come to pass, in other words, facts have here fused with values." [58]

ABRAHAM MASLOW
The Farther Reaches of Human Nature

Not only was it blocking traffic, it wasn't even much of a parade. In fact, it was pathetic. There were Boy Scouts marching out of step and overweight, middle-aged men in out-of-date uniforms. The American flag had seen better days. And the band consisted of some poor soul playing a flute off-key.[59]

Abraham Maslow was driving home from his work at Brooklyn College when he found his progress arrested by the motley procession. The thirty-three-year-old professor was troubled on that fateful day in December of 1941. The Japanese had recently attacked Pearl Harbor and the United States was suddenly at war. Moreover, shortly after the Pearl Harbor disaster, Adolf Hitler had declared war on America. A brooding uncertainty about the future had cast a shadow over the country.

While Maslow watched the tiny parade, something remarkable took place. As he sat there in his car, he was conscious of a growing empathy for the people marching past him, seeking to demonstrate their patriotism. Maslow felt tears begin to run down his face. For some inexplicable reason, he was deeply moved. Then, suddenly, Maslow had a vision of a peace table. Around the table were seated influential people, and they were discussing issues concerning human nature, hatred, and war—as well as the need for peace and brotherhood.

Maslow was having a peak experience. A seemingly trivial event had triggered a vision that would irrevocably alter his life and determine everything he did from that moment on. He realized he now had a lifetime mission, a personal ought-to-be. He would devote himself to discovering a psychology for the peace table. He would strive to prove that human beings are capable of something grander than war, prejudice, and hatred.

Abraham Maslow concluded in those pivotal moments that to achieve his sweeping ought-to-be, he would need to create a new science––a science of values. He decided to challenge the notion that values are the exclusive domain of religionists and visionaries. Maslow was convinced that a science of values could study and explore religion, poetry, and art. He decided that he would strive to understand great people, the best specimens of humankind. He would later write about this peak experience incident and how it inspired the desire in him to study the highest and best achievers. Maslow was determined to discover the secret of their strength and power. That became his mission, his cause … his commitment to something larger and more important than himself.

Fast Forward 25 Years

As he entered the last four years of his life, Abraham Maslow believed he had found the secret he sought. Now he began the arduous task of formulating his discovery into words. He was still working on a formal paper on metamotivation when he spoke publicly about his most important discovery for the first time.

It was perhaps the greatest lecture of his life. But only a handful of students and faculty at the University of Maine heard it. The event was apparently soon forgotten, and his lecture would remain unpublished until thirty years later, long after Maslow's death. On that day in August of 1966, Maslow set his prepared lecture aside and spoke without notes. He seemed to sense that, for him, time was running short, and his "Great Message" was not being heard.

> *"I am just at the point of developing a new theory, and I'm not quite courageous enough to fully accept its implications. It almost frightens me. I am scared of what it may mean in overturning mainstream psychological notions, and it rouses a whole conflict of pride and humility, hubris, and fear. Well, let me try it, and if my voice begins to quiver, you will understand why."* [60]

Maslow then began to review and expand on his ideas regarding his new motivational theory. It was a theory for people who were not crippled by feelings of shame and guilt, mature individuals who were not needy in the traditional sense. But it was beyond being a theory for people who simply had a strong sense of self-worth and were passionately devoted to a cause. Many such people are ruthless, aggressive, and self-centered. Dr. Maslow explained that *metamotivations* is a theory for Self-Actualizers, the one percent of humankind who are *both* devoted to a cause greater than self and dedicated to wholeheartedly embracing MetaValues:

> *"Rather, what constituted the big difference for self-actualizing people was that their activity became a channel or medium for expressing the eternal, ultimate values—the true, the good, the beautiful, the just—in everyday life ... This realization astounded*

me. I remember rereading Plato's Republic, in which he stated that the ultimate good involves the contemplation of the ultimate values. What was so amazing was that I had found men and women in everyday life who were embracing, actually living, these ultimate values … They could be attorneys, educators, scientists, or grocery store owners, but in a real sense, they were sages and saints." [61]

Maslow surveyed the curious but impassive young faces before him.

"… So, I finally have reached a point of thinking: Everyone in this room has a certain degree of saintliness—in the sense of wisdom, of loving justice and being willing to fight for it, of being what is sometimes sneeringly called a 'boy scout' or a 'do-gooder'… one who embodies both wisdom and pragmatism." [62]

Now the reaction came. The young people began to squirm uncomfortably in their seats and shuffle their feet. Maslow smiled. He had expected their embarrassment. The very idea of greatness, or even goodness, causes most people discomfort. Dr. Maslow pressed on. He explained that in the American culture of today, most people are reluctant to think of themselves as noble and kind. They would much prefer to be seen as tough, hard, strong, and never tender-minded about anything. He noted:

"And people often blush when they hear such direct talk. They truly blush, and this is really the only way I know

to get most persons to blush. To ask them about sex won't
do it. But if I ask them to confide their highest motives
and impulses, they probably will begin to blush." [63]

Yet, he noted that if he pursued this line of questioning and "accused" people of loving virtue, they will often admit, "Yes, I would like to bring about such-and-such noble event."

Maslow paused to drink some water. When he looked up at the youthful faces before him, he may have felt a surge of responsibility. There were several curious faces now, regarding him with wonder. He realized he was saying things that few people dared to say, lifting up distinguished ideals that were often regarded as Pollyanna in the academic world. Yet they resonated with many of these students. It seemed they were hungry for an uplifting, optimistic message. *But did they understand the magnitude of what he was saying?*

Maslow continued to speak for a considerable length of time that August morning in Maine. For the first time, he proposed that MetaValues are actually *absorbed* into the psyche of the Self-Actualizer, where they become virtual living realities. They could not be safely removed, no more than a bodily organ could be ripped out without lethal consequences. Dr. Maslow knew that he was now impinging into forbidden territory. He was crossing logic-tight barriers into the realms of philosophy and religion. And he admitted this, to the growing astonishment of his audience. But he was to drive even farther that day with his revolutionary hypothesis that every normal human being was a potential Actualizer. He suggested that a new science of values could produce *metacounselors* who would be trained to understand and teach a new realm of motivation––the realm of *metamotivations*. The idea is that once individuals have acquired enough self-respect or self-worth, they are no longer needy *takers;* they become *givers.*

Maslow acknowledged that what he was recommending constituted a massive paradigm shift. The old Freudian and behaviorist ideas insisted that human nature is infinitely malleable and will become whatever the environment determines it will be. But Maslow declared emphatically that his data indicated otherwise. We are born—all of us—with a natural desire for Truth, Beauty, Goodness, and Love. If these MetaValues are nurtured, vastly greater numbers of children will grow up with the ability to satisfy and eventually transcend deficiency needs and blossom into productive Self-Actualizers. This would have a dramatic impact on civilization.

Maslow gave his all in this lecture. It is as timely and significant today as it was then. But on the long drive back to Brandeis University, he may have realized that he had crossed the professional Rubicon. Not only had he challenged Watson and Freud, he now declared that classic science itself was inadequate to study the higher reaches of human nature. Many colleagues wondered why he would dare such a radical turn. In the words of one of them, Arthur J. Wirth, Chairman, the John Dewey Society Commission on Lectures, "Why should a man hurl his lance against the citadel and risk the rocks and hot oil he may expect in return?" [64] For the short time he had left, Maslow would indeed endure derision from the established academic world. He grew weary of its politics and rigidity. And even though he was gaining some recognition in the business world, Abraham Maslow was not happy with the progress of Third Force psychology. He wondered why so few had elected to expand his research. Maslow lamented that most psychologists who agreed with his work had simply rearranged and reproduced his findings without significant additional investigation.

Psychology 101: Abraham Maslow's Hierarchy of Needs

In the Introduction to this book, I briefly described the 1943 paper that made Dr. Maslow famous, his Hierarchy of Human Needs. This paper proffered a sweeping new concept that forever changed the way we look at human behavior. Maslow noted that there is a logical sequence to the drives that determine our conduct. The strongest drives of all are biological. First, we need air, food, and water. If we are deprived of any of our basic biological needs, nothing else matters until that need is satisfied. Once the biological needs are satisfied, they no longer motivate. A starving man will risk his life for food, but once he is satiated, he will seek the means to protect himself.

What happens when the safety and security issues are satisfied and no longer motivate? Social needs take over. A human being now begins to want to belong, to be appreciated and recognized by others as part of a tribe. What comes next after social wants are reasonably satisfied? An individual wants to stand out from the crowd—to be recognized, special, perhaps even esteemed by others. This need requires some assertiveness, and issues about control and power begin to emerge. Then what? What does an adequately satisfied mortal do at this point? There are no chronic deprivations, or imagined deprivations, to remedy. He or she no longer feels pushed to satisfy a physical or emotional lack.

Now the personality is *pulled* toward a new level of consciousness. The desire to actualize and express self begins to emerge. For the human being, dominated as it is by electrochemical forces and emotional drives, this desire to actualize is at first relatively weak. Even so, this aspiration is very real and triggers MetaValues to stir into action. Maslow represented this hierarchy of needs with a pyramid featuring the strongest and most basic needs at the base, and the ascending needs reaching toward the apex of the pyramid with the arrival of the self-actualizing process *(see Figure Five)*.

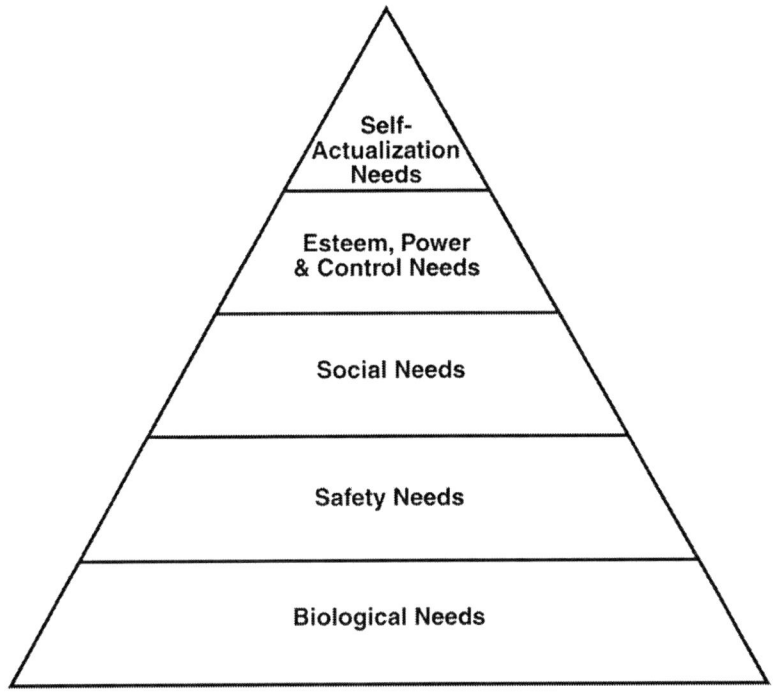

**Figure Five – Abraham Maslow's
Hierarchy of Needs**

Maslow's insights were recognized as remarkable and his hierarchy of needs became generally accepted. But the self-actualizing needs at the top of the pyramid drew resistance from many psychologists. "Values are not the stuff of science," they said. But Maslow insisted that values should not be the sole property of religionists. He urged his colleagues to expand science to embrace values. And Third Force psychology was launched.

You know the rest of that story.

Dr. Maslow's hierarchy of needs has now been around so long that it is a yawner for most students in Psychology 101. Although important progress has been made by many pioneers, the great new frontier of the human mind—the summit of the pyramid—has not yet been fully explored. There is no recognized science of values. And the vast majority of humankind still actualize only a small fraction of their potentials. The time has come to propose a new model of humankind that is based upon Maslow's metamotivation theory—a model that better embraces the farther reaches of what a human being could become.

A New Model of Humankind

Our first step in revising the classic pyramid will be to remove the apex of the pyramid and expand the self-actualizing domain of MetaValues. We will then place a kind of reverse pyramid atop the original. Instead of diminishing to an endpoint, our new model is an egress into a crescendo of the stages of the self-actualizing process, and the unfathomable possibilities for creativity in living at one's highest levels of achievement and service *(see Figure Six)*.

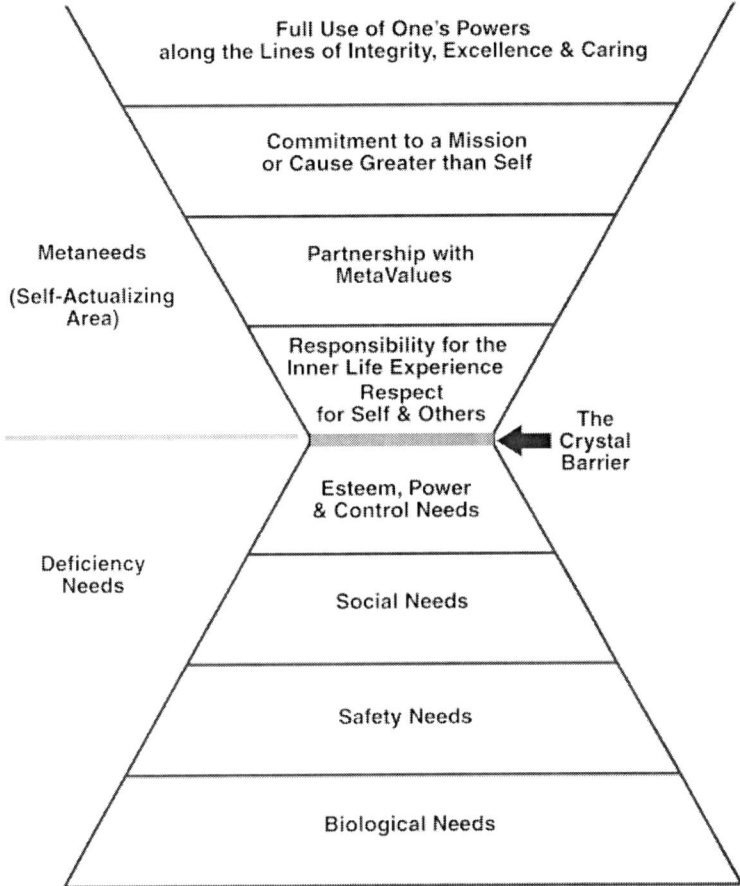

Figure Six – A New Model of Humankind

But note, a crystal barrier, the Will-to-Fail bottleneck, blocks the way. This barrier must be shattered in order to begin a serious exploration of the summit. The early chapters of *The MetaValues Breakthrough* addresses the means of overcoming this barrier by establishing an *impregnable self-respect* and an *uncompromising acceptance of responsibility* for the quality of the inner-life experience. It would be wonderful if we could have a transforming experience and achieve unassailable self-respect and self-confidence in a simple stroke. Or be given the gift of a vision-insight, and transform—in a flash—a hopeless situation into one of meaning and noble purpose. Unfortunately, most of us must do daily grunt work. We must rebuild the edifice of a balanced attitude of confidence and love each day until it becomes a habit. Once this is achieved, a new universe of growth opportunities opens up. We enter into partnership with MetaValues, and this lifts us into a whole new way of living.

54 Minutes That Will Change Your Life

You are now poised to define your mission, your commitment to a cause greater than self. As promised in the previous chapter, you are about to become one of the small percentage of people who have established a working mission for your life, an ought-to-be vision that will continuously inspire and motivate you.

If you followed my recommendations thus far, you have set aside a period to "warm up" each day before you plunge into work. You have done some preliminary work on your grand vision. We will now take this visionary process to yet another level with *54 Minutes That Will Change Your Life*.

We begin with this premise: *When you discover your ultimate mission in life, everything else will fall into place.* You will then be moving toward *becoming* all that you can be, and doing it with maximum expediency. You are on the right bus, and are filling each unforgiving moment with meaning and purpose. And you are doing all of this because a noble idea has found you, and you have fallen in love with it. Without being sought, often many other things are added when the actualization process is fully activated: happiness, health, material prosperity, friends, recognition, influence, etc.

However, if you fail to find your mission, or give up striving to find it, no amount of money, or fame, or power will compensate.

You will likely note that the process I will describe is not established by a laundry list of *what you want*, but rather by creating a clearly defined vision of *what you want to become.* Nor is it based upon a secret system of *getting*, but rather upon the self-discovery of what you have a secret passion to *give*. We will not begin at the beginning, but rather at the conclusion. We are painting a portrait of your vision. Not a step-by-step, from top to bottom, by-the-numbers painting, but rather something created the way a master artist does it, beginning with a vision, and then bringing the entire canvas along simultaneously.

Our primary assumption is that there is a self within to actualize. This is important. If you deny—or even sternly doubt—that there is a higher self to actualize, the process is impeded. If you believe it is too late, that the golden opportunity has been missed, you must suspend this conviction. Granting the existence of a higher self indicates that, on some level, you may already know your mission. A principal purpose of entering the actualization process is to evolve greater awareness of your destiny. *The very fact you have been searching so hard and so long to discover your mission may be evidence that your mission has already found you.*

Phase One: My Ultimate Vision for My Future

We are going to enter into an intense process with several categories. Just use your imagination now, but when you do the written version, it is important that you use no more than the time allotted for each segment.

We will now create a series of visions, each having six distinct facets:

1. My ultimate mission, my gift.

2. My ultimate skills and mental development.

3. My ultimate spiritual development.

4. My ultimate social and family status.

5. My ultimate physical health and appearance.

6. My ultimate material environment.

1. MY ULTIMATE MISSION, MY GIFT (Time limit: 3 minutes). Recall that Viktor Frankl's breakthrough occurred when he saw himself in a comfortable setting, giving a lecture. So imagine your ultimate working area. Make it as extravagant, glamorous, or as challenging as you wish. Imagine the surroundings, the weather, the air, the lighting, the people involved, exactly as you would want it.

Enhance this image until you see yourself working at something you love, something you could eventually learn to do better than anyone else in the world. Think back to something you were working at, or dreamed of doing, for the sheer joy of it, not something you did for someone's approval. Something that resonated deep in your heart. Recall the wonderful sense of freedom and release you felt. Like Frankl, it may be something new, something you want to work at, but never had the opportunity. This is probably a profoundly personal, closely guarded secret you don't dare tell anyone about for fear of ridicule. Besides, even if you had the *will* to pursue it, this calling is far beyond your current *knowledge, skills,* and *means.* And, at this point in your life, you don't have the time or money to acquire them. Do your best to come up with a vision, however weak or fragmented it may be right now. This will be your "working" heart's desire. It will likely evolve as you progress.

2. MY ULTIMATE SKILLS AND MENTAL DEVELOPMENT (Time limit: 3 minutes). Visualize what skills and knowledge will be required for you to achieve your ultimate vision. What skills and knowledge will it take to become a world-class expert or performer in some field? In addition, will you learn a new language or two? Develop a powerful memory for faces and names? Cultivate a Harvard vocabulary? Learn to create a website?

3. MY ULTIMATE SPIRITUAL DEVELOPMENT (Time limit: 3 minutes). Will you be a master at converting each situation to the highest advantage of others? Do you want to develop a connection with a religious community of some kind? Cultivate a remarkable inner-life relationship with God? Better learn to love and serve humankind? Live at your highest level of Integrity, Caring, and Excellence? Imagine what this would be like.

4. MY ULTIMATE SOCIAL AND FAMILY STATUS (Time limit: 3 minutes). What kind of friends and associates will you have? Will you develop a wide area of influence? What kind of family relations will you have? Visualize and describe the type of kindred spirits you will develop relationships with. Will you have a support group of some kind?

5. MY ULTIMATE PHYSICAL HEALTH AND APPEARANCE (Time limit: 3 minutes). Visualize how you would like to look and feel at your best. Will you have a regular exercise program? Will you be eating properly and using quality supplements? Will you be slim, energetic, and active? Will you discard any toxic habits?

6. MY ULTIMATE MATERIAL ENVIRONMENT (Time limit: 3 minutes). Picture in your mind the kind of material setting you would like to be surrounded by someday. What kind of home, in what kind of area would you want if you could choose anything you desired? How would it be furnished? What kind of car would you drive? Imagine the ideal climate, and so on.

The secret of making these visions real is to be as specific as you can today. Use your five senses in these visions. See, smell, touch, taste, and hear all that is contained in your vision. Be honest, but as lavish as your imagination permits.

Total time elapsed: 18 minutes.

Phase Two: My Vision of Myself One Year from Now

1. MY MISSION, MY GIFT (Time limit: 3 minutes). You will have moved in the direction of your dreams and made excellent progress a year from now. Visualize a description of your progress toward your destiny, toward developing your gift to the world as it will appear by this time next year.

2. SKILLS AND MENTAL DEVELOPMENT IN ONE YEAR (Time limit: 3 minutes). Most people believe they do not have time to spend researching and studying in their chosen field. But if it were possible for you to take nine weeks off this year and spend forty uninterrupted, private hours of each of those weeks working on your mission, how much progress do you think you could make? Impossible to get that kind of time off? Perhaps not. I will show you exactly how to do this—regardless of your current circumstances. For now, imagine how much you could accomplish toward world-class Excellence if it were possible to rope out nine forty-hour weeks of uninterrupted personal time to work on your dream.

3. SPIRITUAL DEVELOPMENT IN ONE YEAR (Time limit: 3 minutes). The spiritual factor is very important to maximize your MetaValues success. Remember that science is the domain of *what is* and values are the domain of what *ought to be*. The most neglected MetaValue for materially ambitious people is usually the domain of Goodness, expressed as unconditional respect, or *Caring*. Within one year, what kind of progress can you make toward learning to respect, serve, and love other human beings? Failure to acquire a healthy balance between Caring, Excellence, and Integrity will result in distress and lack of progress.

4. SOCIAL AND FAMILY STATUS IN ONE YEAR (Time limit: 3 minutes). In one year, in what ways and to what degree can you increase your AOI (Area of Influence)? When your candle of world-class excellence is shining as never before, don't hide it under a basket. The world has need of it. Are there any associations you can join? What improvements have you made in your neglected family relationships? Have you become relentless in healing personal grievances and skilled at refusing to be either intimidated or provoked?

5. PHYSICAL HEALTH AND APPEARANCE IN ONE YEAR (Time limit: 3 minutes) Do you have a regular program of exercise? Are you at your ideal weight? Do you get plenty of sleep? Do you schedule regular daily periods of relaxation? Do you have a healthy diet? Have you discarded any toxic habits? Is your wardrobe up to your desired image? Develop a vision of how you will look this time next year.

6. MATERIAL ENVIRONMENT IN ONE YEAR (Time limit: 3 minutes). Create a picture in your mind. This time you want a benchmark vision. What kind of progress do you desire to have made in one year toward the ultimate home you want someday? The area you want to live in? Your income? Describe the complete material status you desire within one year from today.

Total time elapsed: 36 minutes

Phase Three: My Next Steps

What, exactly, are the next steps you can take in each category to energize the MetaValues breakthrough process? A specific next step is easy to figure out. It is the "80" that you have been putting off for a long time. Something you know must be done. Something you have been promising yourself you would do, but keep avoiding. If you find yourself unable to think of a plausible next step in any given category, ask yourself these questions: *Have I been neglecting this area? Can I make my next step an effort to begin to explore this area of my life?* Perhaps your progress has been slowed because you lack balance, and this added facet will exponentially improve the synergy of your performance.

1. MY NEXT STEPS TO TAKE TOWARD MY MISSION, MY GIFT TO THE WORLD (Time limit: 3 minutes). What can I do immediately toward learning more about that thing I am destined to do? What can I do to move in the direction of my dreams?

2. MY NEXT STEPS TO IMPROVE MY SKILLS AND MENTAL DEVELOPMENT (Time limit: 3 minutes). What next-step actions can I take now toward building the personal skills I will need to move toward my one-year goals?

3. MY NEXT STEPS TOWARD SPIRITUAL DEVELOPMENT (Time limit: 3 minutes). If I am on the wrong bus, what next step can I take to get off as soon as possible? Is there any next step I can take to better walk my talk? What next step can I take toward going beyond social conformity toward spiritual action? Can I schedule some time each day for meditative thinking?

4. MY NEXT STEPS TOWARD SOCIAL AND FAMILY STATUS (Time limit: 3 minutes). What next steps can I take now that will move me toward my vision for next year? There are usually several communications that have been put off in families. What can I do to change that in my case?

5. MY NEXT STEPS TOWARD BETTER PHYSICAL HEALTH AND APPEARANCE (Time limit: 3 minutes). Today is the day to start a regular program of exercise. What next step can I take to improve my wardrobe? Or plan a diet? How can I put a power nap into my routine? A fifteen-minute period of meditation to just relax? Or enhance my ultimate mission? What other next steps can I take to improve my nutrition, physical activity, rest, and relaxation?

6. MATERIAL ENVIRONMENT—MY NEXT STEPS (Time limit: 3 minutes). Is there something I can do to improve my physical environment right now? Look around. Can I begin a routine of Kaizen now? (Kaizen is the Japanese philosophy of continuous improvement. The idea is to make each area, without exception, a little better than it was before you leave it, rather than a little worse.) Can I make some favorable addition of sight, sound, taste, touch, and/or smell? What series of steps can I plan immediately to move toward my one-year goal? Review the Pareto Principle presented in chapter seven. Start using it to plan your day, week, and month. "Those who fail to plan—plan to fail."

Total time elapsed: 54 minutes

How to Do It

First, pick a favorable day in the not-too-distant future. Plan to get up early on this day, possibly an hour and a half earlier than usual. Prepare a private area to work. Have handy a cup of coffee, tea, or whatever you need for refreshment. Begin to prepare your worksheets in a notebook of some kind. There are three written phases: Your ultimate vision, your one-year vision, and your next steps. Write in the subcategories. (I strongly recommended that you do this preparation ahead of time). Remember, have a watch at hand; you must not exceed the time limits. Long, tedious goal-writing sessions (as are often implemented in corporations) result in tedious, long-winded goals that no one ever refers to again.

There is enormous significance in getting up early to do the *54 Minutes That Will Change Your Life* process. This is a growth decision of watershed proportions. When you actually get up, you not only break your routine, you also complete your decision. (A decision is never completed until it is acted out.) When you get out of a warm, comfortable bed on this special day, you will do it with the knowledge that few people will be getting up this early on this day by choice. Most people sleep as long as possible and eventually get up because someone else decreed the time they must get up to meet their obligations.

Now, copy the following affirmation, changing it or rewriting it to fit your needs:

> *Today is the most important day of my life. It will be a day that surpasses all other days. Yesterday I cannot change. Tomorrow is a tapestry that will be woven from the threads of today's thoughts and completed decisions. My dreams and visions are just dreams and visions until I act. My highest desires are merely whims until they become priorities. It is through action— completed decisions—that I create my own destiny from moment to moment.*

Read this aloud on the morning you select to formulate your vision. Keep this affirmation. Say it aloud or record it and listen to it every day for several weeks. At some point, you may want to prepare a new one. Some people like to read their affirmations spontaneously each day.

How to Maintain Your Program

Your objective in following these guidelines is to acquire the attitude of a peak performer. If you can do this more effectively by modifying any of the above suggestions, do so. *The important thing is to never begin a day's work until you have achieved an attitude that failure is impossible.* A precious ought-to-be has been assigned to your care, and it is yours to actualize. Never forget that if it truly ought to be, it must be. No force, nor personality, nor circumstance can prevent, nor even long hinder, a MetaValues–driven individual who has been chosen by a genuine ought-to-be.

Maintain your program in the following way:

- ANNUALLY: Repeat the entire *54 Minutes That Will Change Your Life* process.
- AT THE BEGINNING OF EACH MONTH: Set a few specific goals and write them on your calendar.
- WEEKLY: Again, set a few important goals for the week.
- DAILY: Do your Pareto Principle daily plan as described in chapter seven. It is important that you determine whether a task is an "80" or a "20" and that you classify them accordingly. It is equally important that you time-frame each task before you assign it a priority. Finally, prioritize and follow the plan.
- MOMENT TO MOMENT: Much the way a computer monitor must refresh the screen constantly, you must learn the art of stepping aside from the rush of life and pausing to refresh the mind by bathing it with thoughts of Truth, Beauty, and Goodness. *This constant renewing of the mind is a valuable key to peace of mind and productivity.*

If all of this seems like a great deal of trouble, just think of all the time you have wasted because you have not yet formulated a mission and a plan to achieve it. Doing this program is not downtime. As stated before, once your version of this program becomes routine, it will *save* you a great deal of time.

Nine Forty-Hour Weeks of Uninterrupted Time This Year to Work on Your Mission Are Yours for the Taking

For the average under-performer, learning ends after formal education stops. This will not do if you want to become a player on the reality stage of human endeavor. A minimal investment of an hour a day toward new skills will give you an important competitive edge. Why? Because the odds are good that not a single one of your associates will make a commitment of this kind.

One hour each day equals over nine forty-hour weeks a year. In five years, you will have accumulated forty-five work-weeks of research and study. What kind of progress do you imagine you could make if you invested forty-five work-weeks of research and study over the five-year period? Because almost no one does this, you can look forward to some degree of proficiency in a year. In three years, you should be outstanding in your field. In five years, you will have spent over forty-five weeks of effort toward your goals. With any luck at all, you will be world-class.

I strongly suggest that you complete the *54 Minutes That Will Change Your Life* process before you go on to the Epilogue.

EPILOGUE

"When Keats … was transformed from a young lad without a vocation to a young lad who knew that his destiny lay in poetry, he did not think he had changed himself but had been changed, born from above by a vision of a world of beauty he had never sensed before. So all profound transformations of character are associated with the experience, not of lifting oneself, but of being lifted, not of changing oneself but of being changed." [65]

HARRY EMERSON FOSDICK
Riverside Sermons

The MetaValues Breakthrough is not a self-help book, but rather a MetaValues-help book. My premise is not that we can lift ourselves, but rather that we can be lifted. Our difficulties lie in that we know better, but refuse to yield and *allow* ourselves to be lifted. Yield to what? To what we intuitively know to be True, Beautiful, and Good; to act out our lives with nonnegotiable Integrity, Excellence, and Caring. The purpose of this epilogue is to explain how I personally came to believe this as a self-evident truth.

Many years ago, I got on the wrong bus. I thought it would carry me on a journey to independent wealth and happiness. Instead, I ended up in a place of tragedy and despair. There seemed no way out. Then, after many years in a painful wilderness, a simple change of mind allowed me to be lifted out of my situation and be gently placed on the path of a wonderfully new way of life. But, I am getting ahead of my story.

In 1970, I made the fateful decision to leave the gorgeous coastal city of Santa Barbara, California, and move to Tulsa, Oklahoma. I was one of a group of California retail hotshots who planned to build a furniture chain and make millions of dollars. We targeted Tulsa to begin operations because it was a desirable secondary market. We succeeded in the first part of the plan. The Tulsa outlet proved viable and, in a few years, we had a national chain of ten stores, doing the equivalent of a couple hundred million in volume in today's dollars.

To the world, I had chosen the right bus. I had stock in a fast-growing company, a good salary, and a title of Vice President and Director of Marketing. I drove a luxurious Lincoln Mark V and lived in a spacious home. I also had a nice family, including two wonderful daughters. But beneath the surface was the grim truth: *I was in a trap and there were no clear escape routes.* The company I was working for was inhuman and exploitive. I detested my job. I was neglecting my family. As eventually happens with people who get on the wrong bus, I began to look around and wonder: *How did I get to this strange place? Why am I doing things I don't feel good about? Why am I associating with people I don't trust?* Unfortunately, I believed at the time that my options for action were very limited.

Suddenly, a new problem arose. My thirteen-year-old daughter's behavior began to change radically. My sweet, innocent Vicki became a different person almost overnight. I could no longer communicate with her. She began to lie, dress bizarrely, and to associate with unusual new friends. Her grades plummeted. I reacted by denying the symptoms. I told myself this phase would pass. I knew about some of the signs that signaled serious drug problems, but convinced myself that such things only happened to other families. In any event, I believed I needed only to exert willpower to gain control over the situation.

One morning, as I pulled the car out of the driveway to go to work, a piece of trash on the grass outside of Vicki's window caught my eye. I discovered that it was a plastic bag that seemed coated on the inside with dried paint. As I carried the bag inside the house, my mind raced. I had a vague recollection of an activity known as sniffing, the breathing of aerosol can propellants to get a high. I confronted Vicki, and she reluctantly admitted that she was involved with this activity. "It's fun," she said.

What followed was a flurry of ineffective efforts to cope. The Oklahoma school authorities seemed helpless to do much about open drug use and sniffing activities a few feet from school property. There was no reliable place to go for advice. Counseling did not work; none of the existing agencies appeared to be effective. The personnel seemed poorly trained and lethargic. A session with one counselor, a reformed sniffer and drug user, actually did a great deal of harm. Afterward, Vicki said, "He was able to stop and he's OK. He said he tried everything. It didn't hurt him."

Vicki seemed incapable of giving up her compulsion to sniff substances. My wife and I learned that she was experimenting with other drugs. We consulted a prestigious Tulsa psychiatrist who reassured us, and designed a therapy program for Vicki. But by now, she was totally out of control and began leaving the house at night through her window. I became deeply concerned about her physical safety.

The psychiatrist recommended I put Vicki in an expensive treatment center in Tulsa. It was a huge hospital with a sophisticated psychiatric ward. The psychiatrist was confident that under his direction, the controlled milieu, intense therapy, and dedicated staff would help my daughter. Although it was an open ward (patients were not locked up), he told me the professional staff monitored patients carefully. He assured me Vicki would be safe.

Vicki worked with a female associate-therapist on the doctor's staff. The therapist explained to me that the situation with Vicki had exposed severe family dysfunctions. Vicki was the identified family member, the one singled out and blamed for all the things that were wrong with the family in general. In a dysfunctional family, the members generally cooperate in keeping up a facade of tranquility. In our case, my wife and I were hiding a loveless marriage. But continued denial of our problems seemed the easiest course and we were not ready to face the reality of what our marriage had become. One day, after a private session with Vicki's therapist, my wife came home and angrily said, "She asked me if *I* wanted to begin therapy sessions! Can you believe it! What is wrong with that woman?"

About this time, my wife discovered that Vicki had written diaries. Counter to the psychiatrist's advice and her promises to me, my wife read them. She was appalled at the full scope of Vicki's activities. The relationship between the two deteriorated to the point that they could not endure being in the same room. Before long, I was the only one who visited Vicki at the hospital.

I decided to leave my wife, having nursed a secret desire to do so for a long time. My wife suggested that I could bring up Vicki and she could take our other daughter, nine-year-old Kathleen. One morning, when I was putting my clothes in the car, little Kathleen came up to me. She asked where I was going. I told her I was taking a little vacation and would be back soon. That lie would torture me for years to come.

Meanwhile, Vicki became depressed in the hospital. She seemed to feel guilty about the family problems. Her spirits rose when I told her I had arranged to place her in a local children's treatment center, a facility with more intense therapy and dedicated personal attention. There were more young people there and some good peer models. She seemed anxious to get started. The move was delayed a week because an anticipated slot at the new hospital was held up. But I assured Vicki that it would take place in a few more days, just after her fourteenth birthday. When I left her that day, she was in good spirits. She seemed encouraged that in the new treatment center, she would make better progress and could earn more of the freedom she craved.

But the move never happened.

The next afternoon, Vicki and another girl (who also had a sniffing compulsion) managed to talk an attending nurse at the front desk of the psychiatric ward into giving them a plastic bag. The girls went into a room, closed the door, and, for nearly two hours, sniffed aerosol deodorant to get high.

Then a scream came from the room. Vicki had collapsed.

Later that evening, my wife telephoned me at my apartment. She told me the hospital had called. Something was wrong, but they were evasive. I quickly picked her up and drove her there. At the front door of the ward, Vicki's psychiatrist met us. He told us that Vicki Mullins was dead.

Today it is difficult for me to recall many details of the blur of unreality that followed. After the funeral, the full weight of Vicki's death bore down. Vicki, my daughter, the wonderfully talented artist, had vanished. One day I had left her in the hospital ward. In my mind's eye, I could still see her, smiling, waving good-bye to me. The cowboy hat I had just bought her was cocked to one side. Then suddenly all that was left of my little girl was a pathetic shopping cart that the hospital had filled with her belongings and then had called me and asked me to remove. I do remember one other scene clearly. A few months after the tragedy, I knelt at Vicki's gravesite on a chilly, gray morning in November. A light mist was falling. I touched the brutal bronze plaque upon which was etched the reality of the situation:

Vicki Lynn Mullins, Beloved Daughter

1960–1974

I then read aloud a poem I had written to Vicki:

September, '74

Autumn comes now,

trees blaze and winds grow cool and sharp.

But, you cannot awe the colors this year,

> *nor swim in the crisp air.*

Say,

What would you give now,

To taste those awful hospital hamburgers?

To look up at me across the cafeteria table?

To feel my lips good-bye on your cheek?

To hear my warm words, edged with impatience?

Me,

I don't know what I wouldn't give to see you alive again.

But, no matter.

> *You lie below,*

> > *and the leaves blow by,*

> > > *rustling sadly,*

> > > *like a thousand vain regrets of mine.*

My words hung barren and pathetic in the sullen, brooding air. There were no ears to hear them. Or so I believed.

I was a loner with no support system to help me. In desperation, I began to read everything I could find about human behavior, trying to learn what had happened to Vicki. Most of all, I wanted to know if she had somehow survived the death of her body. I came to believe in a religious philosophy that assured me that I would see Vicki again one day. I believed she was now in the care of a benevolent, merciful, personal, parental power of inconceivable magnitude. I imagine, if this story were a Hollywood movie script, the balance of the narrative would describe how I became a saint and learned to serve humanity. But my lessons were barely beginning.

The Aftermath

> *"Many men have thus a secret monster, a disease which they feed, a dragon which gnaws them, a despair which inhabits their night. Such a man resembles other people, goes, comes. Nobody knows that he has within him a fearful parasitic pain, with a thousand teeth, which lives in the miserable man, who is dying of it. Nobody knows that this man is a gulf. It is stagnant, but deep. From time to time, a troubling, of which we understand nothing, shows itself on its surface. A mysterious wrinkle comes along, then vanishes, then reappears; a bubble of air rises and bursts. It is a little thing, it is terrible. It is the breathing of the unknown monster."* [66]

> *VICTOR HUGO*
> *Les Misérables*

In the years that followed, I went through a divorce and lost a painful lawsuit against the hospital. Shortly after the trial ended, Vicki's mother died of the cancer that she had developed less than a year after the devastating loss of her child. I got remarried, perhaps too soon. I was blessed with a beautiful new daughter, Michelle. Finally leaving the corporate world, I began my own marketing and consulting business. I moved to Oklahoma City, ninety miles from the melancholy memories of Tulsa. My daughter, Kathleen, and I worked hard to improve our relationship; slowly, we started getting along. To the world, it may have seemed that I had passed through the tragedy and gone on to do good works. I continued to search for enlightenment and even wrote a few self-help related books. Becoming a somewhat accomplished speaker, I gave seminars on creativity, management, and self-actualization. Yet, down deep in the secret place, I knew something was still terribly wrong.

Within my heart of hearts, I held on to my hatred of the hospital for their negligence and mistakes that led to Vicki's death. Within my inner life lived the venomous resentments I had so long held toward the hospital staff that had permitted Vicki to die and the surgically cold attorneys who had humiliated me in court. Friends who knew about the catastrophe and its aftermath assured me I was justified in harboring resentments. This was well-intentioned but unwise counsel. Because, as we have learned, the law of resentments operates just as inexorably as gravity. There is a price for victimhood.

Then, after eleven years, my second marriage ended. The sudden termination of this relationship hit me with stunning surprise. I wanted a completely new beginning. A close friend suggested that I try group therapy. With a great deal of hesitation––and cynicism––I did so.

The group therapy process was tough. I was required to do something I had never done before: assume an attitude of humility. At one point, participants were required to write and discuss a personal moral inventory. This inventory was to include personal failures and wrongs, character flaws, and harbored resentments. It was at this point that I began to face my own guilt about my relationships with Vicki and her mother. And, as I read over the several pages of anger and resentments I accumulated over the years, I realized that I had to face my own guilt and share of the blame. I came to believe that I was damaged goods. At the same time, I saw no way to repair the damage. The therapy group leader suggested to me that I needed a private session with a more experienced counselor. I agreed, provided I could work with a complete stranger. In a day or so, he gave me the name of an expert counselor in Tulsa.

The Unexpected Peak Experience

So it happened that, fourteen years after Vicki's death, I found myself making the ninety-mile trip from Oklahoma City to Tulsa. As I entered the city that day and drove past the towering hospital, I felt my heart sink in dismay. *That's where they killed Vicki*, I thought. I wanted to turn back to Oklahoma City and forget the whole thing, but I decided to see it through.

It was early afternoon when I reached Ted Wenger's beautiful Tulsa home. Dr. Wenger, a pleasant-looking man in his sixties, was retired. We exchanged a few polite comments as we sat in his comfortable study. He provided me with a cup of fresh coffee, and we prepared to get down to work.

"Dr. Wenger," I said, "before we begin I must tell you something. I know that the purpose of this process is to help heal the resentments I carry within my heart. It is only fair for me to disclose that I have a resentment that not even God could remove. I know this beyond question. So, before we start, I will tell you about it …"

I narrated to him the events of Vicki's death fourteen years before, and its terrible impact upon my life. He listened, his eyes fastened on mine. When I finished, I was surprised that he seemed shaken; his face was white. It took a few moments for him to speak, and I will never forget his words.

"Larry, there is only one place on earth that you should be today and that is here. There is only one person you should be talking to and that is me. What I am about to say astounds me as much as it will you. I am the doctor who led the code blue team that tried to save Vicki's life that night. I remember her vividly. I held her little body in my arms. I thought we had saved her, but then her exhausted heart went into fibrillation and she slipped away. For weeks afterward, I searched our medical library to see if our team had done something wrong, to see if there was a different method that might have been more successful. I satisfied myself finally that we had done all that was humanly possible to save her. But I never forgot her. After I read about the trial, I wanted to meet you, Vicki's father, to tell you these things. And now, at last, I have."

As though moving of its own accord, my hand reached slowly out to his. We sat silently, hand in hand, for what must have been a long time. For us, for an interlude, time did not exist. The mellow afternoon sunlight slanted long across the floor of his study before we spoke again. I remember virtually nothing of what we said.

I did not begin to grasp what had happened until later, when I drove past the hospital again on my way out of Tulsa. The hated building was somehow transformed. Now it stood gilded and beautiful in the late afternoon sun. At that point, clearly in my mind I heard the words: *That's where they tried to save Vicki's life that night.* I don't think anyone actually spoke to me. But it was as though someone had placed a hand upon my shoulder, and gently told me, "My child. Don't tell me what I can or cannot do."

Right then, I realized the incurable pain was gone; I had been completely healed. The resentments and anger were vanished. Later I was to receive a letter informing me that I was not the only one whose life had changed direction after that Tulsa afternoon experience:

> *"On the day you came into my home to talk with me, I had one of those recurring feelings of doubt and dissatisfaction with myself. It was one of those inexplicable and uncomfortable feelings when we doubt whether there is any power willing or even capable of helping us grow in truth and spirit. I can assure you that after our encounter I was a different man, and I have not had doubts nor a negative feeling of that kind since. Oh, yes, I've had my ups and downs, but I perceive that experience as a turning point in my life, and an important one. I have told of our meeting from my own perspective in several meetings and it never fails to amaze and inspire many, and even 'spook' a few."*
>
> *Dr. Theodore Wenger*
> *Tulsa, Oklahoma*

I had been unaware that I was struggling under immense burdens until the weight of my resentments lifted. I was also free of the encumbrance of guilt. The endless struggle to "fix" myself was over. I no longer shamefully thought of myself as damaged goods. Now, in one peak experience moment, the possibilities seemed endless. With this new clarity came the sense that what I was seeking all these years had always been near at hand. At the time, I thought that I had been given a special gift that afternoon in Tulsa. But I was to learn that virtually all normal people have such experiences.

Chopping Wood and Carrying Water

Even so, my search was not over, but rather renewed at a more advantageous spiritual level. I was to learn that even dramatic peak experiences—by themselves—do not necessarily change lives. It is rather what one does with these gifts that matters. There is an ancient Chinese saying: *Before enlightenment, chopping wood and carrying water. After enlightenment, chopping wood and carrying water.* And so it has been with me. The memory of that afternoon in Tulsa remained vivid, and my life began to improve. However, the peak *feeling* of joy, completeness, and limitless energy began to fade.

The agony of the resentments I carried was gone, but boredom and anxiety gradually returned to dominate my life. *Why?* I wondered. *Why couldn't I maintain that sense of total renewal—that grasp of a higher reality that I had when I left Tulsa and saw the hospital I hated transformed into something of wonder and beauty? Why couldn't I make that extraordinary level of consciousness return to stay? Or, at least a meaningful degree of that fleeting, powerful, glad-to-be-alive feeling?* I am convinced that the concept of MetaValues provides part of the answer to these questions. Maslow believed that MetaValues are somehow biologically based and a pathway toward optimal mental health. For me, they became a pathway to an experience of God on a new level.

The grand premise of *The MetaValues Breakthrough* is that, to the degree that we strive for greater and greater expression of the True, the Beautiful, and the Good, we are lifted by the most powerful forces in the universe. We are lifted because we are in tune with the purpose of the creator of the universe. One cannot have a relationship with biology. And Maslow seemed to perceive this when he wrote in his journals, late in his life:

> "*It's no longer controllable. I must go the way I must go … I'm contributing what no one else can & what I rationally believe ought to be written about. Most important thing I can do is write my ideas about science, about B-psychology, about metamotivation, etc. If there were an all-wise dictator someplace, that's what he'd order me to do.*" [67]

Even so, the complete answer cannot be found in the pages of any book. The greatest story of all will be lived, not written. It will be the story you reveal to the world as you live out your life. Don't imagine that you must begin with a world-changing vision to set the self-actualizing process into motion. Viktor Frankl had a modest vision of his destiny when he was trapped in a Nazi death camp. Doubtless, the Nazi guards would have laughed at his vision. But long after the Nazis of that day drifted into shame and oblivion, the legacy of Frankl's journey lives on.

Whatever dream burns in your heart today may also seem laughable to some who underestimate you, considering the odds against it. Believe your dream all the more. Your dream is more important than any material priority. In the meantime, whatever is placed before you, engage it with all your heart and soul. Being a great teacher, a great mother or father, or even a great neighbor—any endeavors that change other lives are worthy and important self-actualizing goals.

May you become one of those rare, pragmatic visionaries who have the realistic insight to see life as it is, and also the poetic and spiritual vision to see life as it ought to be. And, may you do even more than dream of things that ought to be. May you become one of those even rarer actualizers who dare to move in the direction of those dreams, knowing that *anything, absolutely anything that ought to be actualized must be actualized.* Circumstances may seem to impede, but they cannot prevent.

Each wholehearted effort to contact the source of the True, the Beautiful, and the Good will be successful. We are all in this together, including the "all-wise dictator."

Persist, find, yield, and be *lifted.*

About the Author

Larry Mullins is the President and CEO of UltraSales, Inc., providing management consulting and syndicated internet-based marketing programs to retailers nationwide. He has conducted graduate school classes on creativity and personal development around the country. Larry has written a number of motivational books, including *Immature People with Power—How to Handle Them, Sixty-Two Minutes that will Change your Life, Goal Setting for Women Only,* and *Get Real.* He lives in St. Augustine, Florida, with his wife, Joan.

Acknowledgments

First and foremost, thanks to my wife, Joan, who is a dedicated student of MetaValues. Joan taught me that in order to learn about Truth, Beauty, and Goodness, we must first *love* what is true, beautiful, and good. Because of her faith, precious counsel, and patient editing, *The MetaValues Breakthrough* became a reality. Thanks to Dr. Jill Strump, Dr. Meredith J. Sprunger, and Special Forces Sgt. First Class Pat Sonti for reading the manuscript and offering important insights. Thanks to Tony Edens, who provided wisdom, guidance, and most of all, friendship throughout the long ride. Thanks to Lou Aronica for doing his magic touches with the text, and to my agent John Willig for his vision and key suggestions. Finally, my gratitude to David and Ben Hancock of Morgan James Publishing for daring to publish this breakthrough book.

An Invitation to Connect and Share Your MetaValues Insights …
Each person reading this book has the potential to achieve uncommon levels of genius, success, and happiness. The recipe is simple: *full use of your powers along the lines of Integrity, Caring, and Excellence toward a cause or mission that you love.* No special training is needed to begin this experiment. The laboratory is life itself. Before you close this book, consider taking part in bringing the MetaValues message to the world. At *www.metavalues.net* you will find an invitation to …

The MetaValues® Connection

The MetaValues Connection is an informal community of individuals of diverse backgrounds and persuasions who share the core MetaValues of *Truth, Beauty,* and *Goodness.* Beyond sharing these values, we also strive to make them visible through uncompromising *Integrity*, dedicated *Excellence*, and unconditional *Caring* and respect. Laypersons, religionists, scientists, and philosophers will all find common ground here. Our mission is nothing less than to change the world.

I strongly urge you to introduce these concepts to your own circle of friends. Consider giving kindred spirits a copy of this book. Join our MetaValues Connection family by telling others how MetaValues have touched your life. If you have your own website or blog, consider sharing your MetaValues experiences there.

Write a review of *The MetaValues Breakthrough* for your newspaper or post it on www.amazon.com. Ask your company, college, or association to invite Larry Mullins as a guest speaker. Visit our website, www.metavalues.net, to get free information, downloads of inspiring material, and to learn more about MetaValues Connection activities and opportunities.

NOTES

1. Quoted in: F. G. Goble, *The Third Force, The Psychology of Abraham Maslow* (New York: Pocket Books, 1975), Back Cover.

2. Quoted in: A. H. Maslow with D. C. Stevens and G. Heil, *Maslow on Management* (New York: John Wiley & Sons, Inc., 1998), Back Cover.

3. Ibid, Back Cover.

4. A. H. Maslow, *The Maslow Business Reader,* ed. Deborah C. Stephens (New York: John Wiley & Sons, Inc., 1998), viii.

PREFACE

5. C. Wilson, *New Pathways in Psychology, Maslow & the Post-Freudian Revolution* (New York: Taplinger Publishing, Inc., 1972), 183.

6. C. Hitchens, *god is Not Great, How Religion Poisons Everything* (New York: Twelve, Hachette Book Group, USA, 2007), 12.

7. Ibid., 12.

8. A. H. Maslow, *The Psychology of Science, a Reconnaissance* (Chicago: A Gateway Edition, 1970), 119.

INTRODUCTION

9. Quoted in: A. H. Maslow with D. C. Stevens and G. Heil, *Maslow on Management* (New York: John Wiley & Sons, Inc., 1998), 3.

10. A. H. Maslow, *Motivation and Personality* (New York: Harper & Row, 1970), 180.

11. C. Wilson, *New Pathways in Psychology, Maslow & the Post-Freudian Revolution* (New York: Taplinger Publishing, Inc., 1972), 183.

12. Ibid., 184.

CHAPTER ONE

13. A. H. Maslow, *Religions, Values, and Peak Experiences* (New York: Penguin, 1994), 64–65.

14. A. H. Maslow, *The Farther Reaches of Human Nature* (New York: The Viking Press, 1971), 339. Copyright © 1971 by Bertha G. Maslow. Viking Penguin, a division of Penguin Group (USA) Inc.

15. L. Lederman with Dick Teresi, *The God Particle, If the Universe is the Answer, What is the Question?* (New York: Delta, 1993), 384.

16. A. H. Maslow, *Motivation and Personality* (New York: Harper & Row, 1970), 165.

17. A. H. Maslow, with D. C. Stephens and G. Heil, *Maslow on Management* (New York: John Wiley & Sons, Inc., 1998), 122.

18. R. Stone Zander and B. Zander, *The Art of Possibility* (Boston: Harvard Business School Press, 2000), 19–20.

CHAPTER TWO

19. A. H. Maslow, *The Farther Reaches of Human Nature* (New York: The Viking Press, 1971), 35–36. Copyright ©1971 by Bertha G. Maslow. Viking Penguin, a division of Penguin Group (USA) Inc.

20. D. Brande, *Wake Up and Live! A Formula For Success That Works* (New York: Cornerstone Library, 1936), xiii–xv.

21. A. J. Cronin wrote two versions of his life-transforming experience. Each version contains unique information important to the story, so both were used in creating the new version in *The MetaValues Breakthrough*.

    "Getting the Most Out Of Life" (anthology), A. J. Cronin, *The Turning Point of My Career* (Pleasantville, NY: The Reader's Digest Association, 1946), 1–6.

    "Light From Many Lamps" (anthology), A. J. Cronin, *The Virtue of All Achievement is Victory over Oneself. Those Who Know this Victory Can Never Know Defeat* (New York: Simon and Schuster, 1951), 147–151.

22. M. Csikszentmihalyi, *Flow, The Psychology of Optimal Experience* (New York: Harper & Row, 1990), 3. Copyright © 1990 by Mihaly Csikszentmihalyi. HarperCollins Publishers.

23. J. Cavanaugh, *Tunney, Boxing's Brainiest Champ and His Upset of the Great Jack Dempsey* (New York: Random House, 2006), 263.

24. Ibid., 300.

CHAPTER THREE

25. F. G. Goble, *The Third Force, The Psychology of Abraham Maslow* (New York: Washington Square Press, 1970), 33.

26. M. Collins and C. Tamarkin, *Marva Collins' Way, Return to Excellence in Education and Quality in the Classrooms* (Los Angeles: Jeremy P. Tarcher, Inc., 1982), 22 & 75.

27. Ibid., 106.

28. Ibid., 137.

29. W. Beecher and M. Beecher, *Beyond Success and Failure, Ways to Self-Reliance and Maturity* (New York: Pocket Books, 1975), 33–34.

30. A. H. Maslow, *Religions, Values, and Peak Experiences* (New York: Penguin, 1994), 20–21.

31. Ibid., vii–viii.

CHAPTER FOUR

32. J. Allen, *As A Man Thinketh* (Old Tappan, NJ: Fleming H. Revell Company), 11–12.

33. Viktor Frankl's story is derived from six original sources:

   V. Frankl, *Man's Search for Meaning* (New York: Washington Square Press, 1984).

   V. Frankl, *The Doctor and the Soul, From Psychotherapy to Logotherapy* (New York: Vintage Books, 1983).

V. Frankl, *Man's Search for Ultimate Meaning* (New York: Insight Books, 1997).

V. Frankl, *Recollections, An Autobiography* (New York: Insight Books, 1997).

D. Schultz, *Growth Psychology, Models of the Healthy Personality* (New York: D. Van Nostrand Company, 1977).

H. Klingberg, Jr., *When Life Calls Out to Us, The Love and Lifework of Viktor and Elly Frankl* (New York: Doubleday, 2001).

34. V. Frankl, *Man's Search for Meaning* (New York: Washington Square Press, 1984), 133–134.

35. Ibid., 88–89.

36. The story of Buckminster Fuller's transformation is based upon an interview by John Love in *QUEST 79*, Nov./Dec. 1979.

37. A. Fuller Snyder, "Experience and Experiencing," www.thirteen.org.

38. D. Wasserman and J. Darion, *Man of La Mancha* (New York: Random House, 1966), 60–61. Copyright © 1966 by Dale Wasserman. Used by permission of Random House, Inc.

CHAPTER FIVE

39. P. F. Drucker, *Managing Knowledge Means Managing Oneself* (Leader to Leader, No. 16, Spring, 2000), 8–10.

40. Yogi Ramacharaka, *Raja Yoga, or Mental Development* (Chicago, IL: The Yogi Publication Society, 1934), 1.

41. Ibid., 42–43.

42. W. Beecher and M. Beecher, *Beyond Success and Failure, Ways to Self-Reliance and Maturity* (New York: Pocket Books, 1975), 14.

CHAPTER SIX

43. P. Russell, *The Brain Book* (New York: E. P. Dutton, 1979), 5. Copyright © 1979 by Peter Russell. Dutton Signet, a division of Penguin Group (USA) Inc.

44. J. Steinbeck, *Journal of a Novel, The East of Eden Letters* (New York: The Viking Press, 1969), Dust Jacket.

45. R. Dallek, *An Unfinished Life … John F. Kennedy 1917–1963* (New York: Little, Brown and Company, 2003), 33.

46. *Thank You, Mr. President, The JFK Press Conference Highlights,* World Vision Home Video, Inc., 1983. (video)

47. Anonymous, *The Urantia Book* (Chicago, 1955), 1435.

48. J. F. Kennedy, *In Our Own Words, Extraordinary Speeches of the American Century, Tribute to Robert Frost,* ed. R. Torricelli and A. Carroll (New York: Washington Square Press, 1999), 242–243.

49. H. E. Fosdick, *Riverside Sermons* (New York: Harper & Brothers, 1958), 5.

CHAPTER SEVEN

50. M. Csikszentmihalyi, *Flow, The Psychology of Optimal Experience* (New York: Harper & Row, 1990), 3. Copyright © 1990 by Mihaly Csikszentmihalyi. HarperCollins Publishers.

51. A. H. Maslow, *The Farther Reaches of Human Nature* (New York: The Viking Press, 1971), 65–67. Copyright © 1971 by Bertha G. Maslow. Viking Penguin, a division of Penguin Group (USA) Inc.

52. C. A. Garfield with H. Zina Bennett, *Peak Performance, Mental Training Techniques of the World's Greatest Athletes* (Los Angeles, CA: Warner Books, 1984), based on Dr. Garfield's experience with the Soviets in Milan on pages 17–19.

53. Ibid., 19.

54. Ibid., 21.

55. C. Garfield, *Peak Performers, the New Heroes of American Business* (New York: Avon, 1986), 304. Copyright © 1986 by Charles Garfield. HarperCollins Publishers.

56. A. Robbins, *The Power to Shape Your Destiny! Seven Strategies for Massive Results* (Robbins Research International, 2001), promotional material.

CHAPTER EIGHT

57. V. E. Frankl, *Man's Search for Ultimate Meaning* (New York: Insight Books, 1997), 40.

58. A. H. Maslow, *The Farther Reaches of Human Nature* (New York: The Viking Press, 1971), 108–109.

59. "The Psychology Of Universality," *Psychology Today*, Vol. 2, No. 2, July 1968.

60. A. H. Maslow, *Future Visions, The Unpublished Papers of Abraham Maslow*, ed. E. Hoffman (Thousand Oaks, CA: Sage Publications, 1996), 89.

61. Ibid., 90–91.

62. Ibid., 91.

63. Ibid., 91.

64. Quoted in Foreword to A. H. Maslow, *The Psychology of Science, a Reconnaissance* (Chicago: A Gateway Edition, 1970), x.

EPILOGUE

65. H. E. Fosdick, *Riverside Sermons* (New York: Harper & Brothers, 1958), 79–80.

66. V. Hugo, *Les Misérables* (New York: Barnes & Noble, Inc., 1996), 1187.

67. A. H. Maslow, *The Journals of Abraham Maslow*, ed. R. J. Lowry (Lexington, MA: The Lewis Publishing Company, 1982), 100.

BUY A SHARE OF THE FUTURE IN YOUR COMMUNITY

These certificates make great holiday, graduation and birthday gifts that can be personalized with the recipient's name. The cost of one S.H.A.R.E. or one square foot is $54.17. The personalized certificate is suitable for framing and will state the number of shares purchased and the amount of each share, as well as the recipient's name. The home that you participate in "building" will last for many years and will continue to grow in value.

Here is a sample SHARE certificate:

HABITAT FOR HUMANITY

THIS CERTIFIES THAT

YOUR NAME HERE

HAS INVESTED IN A HOME FOR A DESERVING FAMILY

1985-2005

TWENTY YEARS OF BUILDING FUTURES IN OUR
COMMUNITY ONE HOME AT A TIME

1200 SQUARE FOOT HOUSE @ $65,000 = $54.17 PER SQUARE FOOT
This certificate represents a tax deductible donation. It has no cash value.

YES, I WOULD LIKE TO HELP!

I support the work that Habitat for Humanity does and I want to be part of the excitement! As a donor, I will receive periodic updates on your construction activities but, more importantly, I know my gift will help a family in our community realize the dream of homeownership. **I would like to SHARE in your efforts against substandard housing in my community!** *(Please print below)*

PLEASE SEND ME _____ SHARES at $54.17 EACH = $ $_____

In Honor Of: _____

Occasion: (Circle One)   *HOLIDAY*   *BIRTHDAY*   *ANNIVERSARY*

       OTHER: _____

Address of Recipient: _____

Gift From: _____ *Donor Address:* _____

Donor Email: _____

I AM ENCLOSING A CHECK FOR $ $_____ **PAYABLE TO HABITAT FOR HUMANITY** OR PLEASE CHARGE MY VISA OR MASTERCARD *(CIRCLE ONE)*

Card Number _____ Expiration Date: _____

Name as it appears on Credit Card _____ Charge Amount $ _____

Signature _____

Billing Address _____

Telephone # Day _____ Eve _____

PLEASE NOTE: Your contribution is tax-deductible to the fullest extent allowed by law.
Habitat for Humanity • P.O. Box 1443 • Newport News, VA 23601 • 757-596-5553
www.HelpHabitatforHumanity.org

Printed in the United States
150063LV00010BA/129/P